WHAT HAUNTS US

A Story Collection
by Loren Niemi

Thanks John for your contribution!!

Moonfire Publishing

Also by Loren Niemi

Inviting the Wolf In:
Thinking About Difficult Stories

The New Book of Plots

Coyote Flies Coach

(612) 200-3359
www.moonfire-publishing.com

Published in 2019 by Moonfire Publishing
Cover Design by Scott Stenwick
Cover Photo by Loren Niemi
Author Photo by JoAnn Niemi

ISBN: 0-9993744-4
ISBN-13: 978-0-9993744-4-3

In memory of

Hannah Chance Niemi
Bobbie Niemi Kurth
Don Byrne
Melisande Charles

The spirits always close at hand

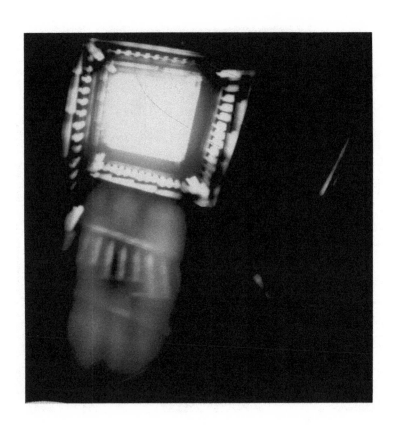

"WHAT HAUNTS US are those things we hold in memory or in feelings: people, geography, actions, philosophies and beliefs, and emotions themselves. I have lived with some of these stories for decades. Giving them the form that they deserved eventually became inevitable.

This collection includes the reworking of oral histories that give a nod to testimony of ghosts and the metaphysical, narratives that explore the ways in which we make the intangible present, and finally the tale of the Count Saint Germain, which is about how grief haunts even immortals."

– Loren Niemi

Contents

Fishhook

UP ON MINNESOTA'S Gunflint Trail there is a certain comfortably run-down resort where the third cabin on the left, the one by the dock, was once the scene of a terrible death. No, I won't tell you which outfit it was. That'd be bad for business, but I will tell you what happened.

Old Doctor Morrison came up from Chicago to retire. He had to. While he was a fair to middlin' surgeon he was also a better than middlin' drinker. One malpractice suit too many prompted a relocation and the Boundary Waters seemed just far enough away. So, he settled down in that cabin in the resort on the Gunflint Trail and began fishing day in and day out. He fished about as good as he doctored, but since he pretty much kept to himself so as to not be a burden on his neighbors, no one really cared how much he fished or drank.

Anywise, there's this one time Doc Morrison got himself a couple of good ones off the point. Walleyes, if I remember right. Caught the two of 'em and probably had a few sips of the good stuff while he was waiting for something else to bite. Had a few more nips off the flask every time he pulled those beauties in to celebrate the catch. When he tied the boat to the dock, he was wobbling. Took them fish back to the cabin, put one on ice and filleted one to cook up for supper. Probably had a few more sips along the line, 'cause he did a real sloppy job with that old Rapala fish knife. He must have left half the flesh on the table. A bunch of bone was included with the meat that did go into the fry pan, but since he didn't leave any fingers on the cutting board, in his estimation he couldn't have been that drunk.

Cooked it up real nice and sat down to eat. Fresh walleye filets and some sliced yellow potatoes. But he got not more than two or three bites into it and he gets a bone stuck in his throat.

Now some say it was a fishhook, but even drunk, you'd think a man would have the sense to not eat a fishhook. Whatever it was, it gets lodged in his throat and he can't cough it out.

He's choking, grabbing for things, knocking the plate off the table, turning blue, gasping for air. It's bad. Really bad. So Doc turns to his medical training to save himself. He gets hold of the Rapala knife and inserts it down through his mouth and into his gullet. Just plunges the blade in and wiggles it around till he feels the bone, or the fishhook, and tries to cut it out. Must've hurt like hell. Blood was spilling everywhere.

He goes to take a drink to ease the pain but the booze just runs straight from his mouth out a hole in his neck. Maybe he goes for another swallow, maybe he just passes out and falls to the floor, where he proceeds to bleed out. But by the time they find him, he's been dead for a good week. Bloated carcass, flies everywhere, and the whole cabin stinks of rotting fish, blood, and booze. It was an awful mess.

They really should have burned the cabin down to the ground, right then and there. But the guy who owns the resort wouldn't do it. Cleaned the cabin as best could be done and rented it out again. He figures he can skate on by.

But when new folks rented the place, they weren't there a day or two before they was complaining of a nasty wet spot in the kitchen. A slippery patch with a red stain that wouldn't dry no matter how much blotting or mopping or scrubbing they did. They said it smelled of booze and something they couldn't quite name. The management moved them out and tried to rent it again. Same thing happened to the next folks. And the ones after that.

Finally, the resort owner was forced to tear out the flooring. Put new hardwood in and rented the cabin again. Even with the new floor it was the same story. Always a complaint about a dark wet spot in the kitchen and the smell of something gone very wrong.

One of these times he'll finally get tired of complaints and burn the cabin down like he should have done when Doc did himself in. Or maybe he'll sell the land and be done with it. Meanwhile, the locals watch the parade of city folks in and out. Anyone who knows better knows enough not to rent that third cabin by the dock.

George, Henry & Marguerite

IN THE PERPETUAL twilight of the beer signs inside the Deer River VFW they looked even older than their eighty-some years. George with tufts of white hair coming out of his ears, eyebrows a snow-covered hedge over still bright green eyes, his face a field of wrinkles. He sat with his fist wrapped around a bottle. Marguerite was without a trace of make-up or primping, except for her white hair in a style that would have been fashionable in the '50's. She held a glass of foamy Grain Belt beer and listened while George told me the history of the town.

Plain folks, they were. Plain spoken. As I sat with them and as I listened, however, I realized the story George and Marguerite had to tell was anything but plain, even though they might have said it in the simplest of words.

George and his brother, Henry, were identical twins born in the last year of the nineteenth century on the farm George still owned and only recently stopped working. They had grown up on those 60 acres of land, with no electricity, no running water. The brothers both received their primary education in a one room schoolhouse. When the Great War broke out, they were still in high school. In a patriotic fever they joined the American Expeditionary Forces as soon as they were of an age to volunteer. Gone to France, they saw Paris both before and after they saw the trenches and death in abundance.

Of the thirty-two men who left Deer River for that great conflict, only six lived to see the homecoming tears of their family and friends. George and Henry lived through the war and came back to do the only thing they thought would calm their shattered nerves, to toil with their father on the farm. Even after their father died, they worked the seasons with the habits of discipline their father and the Lutheran faith had instilled in them. They even slept in the same bedroom they had shared as boys.

The farm flourished. They did well enough to replace the horse and wagon with a Model A truck. They bought a tractor too and strung an electric line to the house and to the barn. They were frugal as well, and when the Depression arrived, they had enough saved to not go under and continued on as if time, and not money, was the scarcest commodity.

In 1933, Henry woke up one November morning and seeing that the crops were in and the fallow season was about to commence, he decided that it was time to get married. He told his brother George that he had been a bachelor long enough. For whatever reason, none of the local girls would do, so Henry caught a train all the way to Saint Paul, where he was sure to find a wife. When he came back in time to begin spring planting as he had promised, his newly married wife, Marguerite was by his side.

So, they all settled in. Henry and Marguerite took the father's bedroom and the double bed with the creaky springs. George kept the one he had shared with his brother since birth. The three of them drank coffee together in the kitchen in the morning and read the Bible or the Farmer's Almanac together at night. On Saturday evenings, they might go into town to the VFW for a little socializing, and then Sundays they dressed for church, the brothers wearing the clean white shirts that Marguerite had washed and pressed for them.

That's how it went for forty-two years. Then Henry died, and George and Marguerite were left with each other.

George excused himself and got up to go to the men's room. While he answered nature's call, I asked Marguerite if it was difficult living day in and day out with the image of her departed husband. She said, "No, it is actually a comfort for me, but I'll tell you the truth, it is very hard on George. When Henry died, he was like a man who had lost his shadow."

When George came back, we drank another round without much conversation between the three of us. Then Marguerite got up to the Ladies' room and while she was away, I asked George how it was living with his brother's wife. "Oh," he said in a voice as flat as the beer he was nursing, "We get on pretty well. It was hard at first. We were both pretty lonely. But things are better now that Henry's ghost comes to visit."

The words were so matter of fact that I was tempted to let it slide as an old man's joke, a wishful remark. He saw my skepticism and leaned closer. "You know, what's funny about that ghost? Some nights he sleeps in her bed, and then sometimes he slips into mine just like we were ten years old again."

The hour was late, and they took their leave to drive the four miles to the 60 acres that had always been enough. I sat in the booth listening to the juke box playing Sinatra, overhearing the young couple at the next table negotiating a sex act with a friend that I did not believe would have shocked George, Henry or Marguerite but which I very much doubted they had ever done. When the threesome left, I followed them out the door. They turned towards the parking lot and I crossed the street to my car.

It took a good twenty minutes to drive to where I figured the farm was. Neither George nor Marguerite had given me a mailbox number but there were not many places along this road. Based on what they had said, I came to a little rise and saw the house with their car parked in front.

I didn't go in. It was much too late to visit. What would I say or expect to see? Instead I was content to sit there with the lights off, the engine running and watched the house lamps go dark one by one as they settled for the night. George would be in his room and she in hers across the hall.

And Henry? Where would he be? I could imagine the shimmer of spirit standing in the hallway, deciding where to turn on this night. Which would want, which would need, the comfort of the one who was still very much alive though not in the body? I smiled at the thought of a ghost that cared so much, turned my headlights on and put the car in gear. It would be a long drive to where I was staying. Unfortunately no one would be waiting for my return.

Memorial Day

IT WAS MEMORIAL DAY weekend in 1969. A Memorial Day weekend just north of Ely at the thin edge of the boundary waters. A weekend with six college buddies who were supposed to be having vacation fun. This proved to be difficult at best, since we were all trapped in a tent with the rain coming down.

We had gotten as far as the first campsite on Thursday when the rain began. The idea of going further in that downpour was unappealing and so we settled in, thinking that it would clear the next day. Three days later, the rain was still coming down. The prospect of a glorious summer weekend in the wilderness had been completely washed away. We'd been through everything we packed to read, every card game we could think of to play, and then we realized that when we ran out of food, we'd have to make a day's paddle back on an empty stomach. To escape that fate, we tried to fish while ignoring the rain, which left us mostly wet and cranky, but with a few scrawny crappies to show for our efforts. We ultimately passed through the nothing better to do stage and began sleeping a lot, which was better than the sniping, arguing and acute awareness of each other's annoying habits we increasingly indulged in when we were awake.

I was not a happy camper. None of us were.

So, we decided to pack it up and go back to Ely that Monday morning, rain or no rain. We loaded the canoes at first light and settled in for a four, five, maybe six-hour paddle in what was now a light drizzle. After three full days of rain, though, our clothes never had a chance to dry out. Given how wet we were, even a light drizzle was bringing us to the miserable edge of hypothermia.

When the sight of the first cabins in the town of Ely arose through the wet washed gray landscape, it was as if we were seeing the Promised Land. When we pulled the canoes onto the landing and loaded the soaked everything into our cars, all I could think of was to find someplace dry and warm, where I could have a good stiff whiskey. I was so focused on my clammy clothes and water-logged boots that I actually passed by the first bar I came to without noticing it – but not the second one.

It might have been called the Dew Drop Inn or something else. Walking through the door I found a classic dive bar with stuffed deer heads and lacquered fish on the walls. Posters announcing dances and wrestling matches hung next to the entry. A bald bartender wearing a green plaid shirt was serving bumps and brews to a bunch of morose bikers.

It had not of occurred to me that the Harleys outside might have been there for as long as we were paddling. It seemed they were entertaining themselves playing variations of mumblety-peg involving the insertion of the blade of a sharp knife between the outstretched fingers of the hand. If you flinched, you had to buy a round. Survey the room and you'd see tabletops covered with nicks, blood stains, and every one of those boys seemed to be intoxicated to half past zombie as they sucked gashed fingers and Jim Beam.

One of them caught my eye and gave me the dirty look that redneck bikers reserved for long-hair college kids in that year, which was, in fact, exactly what I was. In those days the typical Midwestern biker embraced a flag waving, napalm-the-whole-dammed-place-to-ashes kind of blind patriotism, untainted by the complexities of the political change posited by college intellectuals or the remorseful admonitions of returning Vietnam vets.

I turned to go but it was already too late. The hoarse cry of "FRESH MEAT!" rang out from the depths of the assembled company. In the blink of an eye I was grabbed and pushed into a chair. I looked across the table. Directly in front of me sat a larger than life biker with the name 'Tiny' embroidered on his blue jean jacket.

Why would anyone persist in the false irony of naming a six-foot-four-inch, three to four-hundred-pound hairless gorilla 'Tiny?'

He was sitting there with a few missing teeth behind a big smile and a six-inch ebony handled blade at the ready. The man who had sat me down was holding my hand to the table and whispered to me, *Spread them wide!*

Which I took to be sage advice in that moment.

I thought of the guys when we were back in the tent bitching at each other about burned hash browns and weak coffee. I missed that time and place already. So what if we had no fish to show for our sojourn – that was better than this. There were some kinds of Northwoods adventures I could do without.

Tiny raised his knife. There was a glint in his eye as if he was looking at something far away. Suddenly the knife dropped to the floor, his mouth fell open, and a little trail of spittle began running down his chin. His head rolled back as if there was something on the ceiling that he had just noticed. His body jerked like he had touched a live wire, stiffening, tipping the chair as he went backward. Gravity took hold and he followed the knife to the floor, his feet catching and then kicking the table over.

I jumped up, backed away from the mass of Tiny lying there. The bikers weren't paying attention to me anymore. They crowded around the unmoving form. His denim jacket with the cut off sleeves lay open, revealing a Confederate flag sewn in as a lining. Whether it was merely decoration or some fundamental loyalty I can't say.

Tiny, are you all right? They called to him. One of them lifted his head, cradling Tiny in his lap, stroking his cheek. It looked like a strange variation on Michelangelo's famous statue of the Virgin Mary holding Jesus' body. Like a biker version of La Pieta. Someone must have called the cops or an ambulance, because I heard a siren getting closer.

I suppose I could have stayed to watch what happened next, but seeing the flag on the inside of his jacket got me thinking about the blue and the gray origins of Memorial Day. Here in a tavern in the far north of the Union, it was the stars and stripes that were on display. The stars and bars of the defeated South were seldom seen where the Union dead rested.

Tiny, the bearer of that fallen battle flag who I presumed was loyal to the defeated South, had been struck down like so many sons and brothers in the war that would have ended America. I remembered reading one estimate of 627,00 dead in the Civil War. More deaths than all of the other wars America has sent sons to die in – Vietnam, Korea, the Big One, the War to End All Wars. Imagine one quarter of all males between the ages of 16 and 40 killed, with almost as many dying of disease as bullets in a four-year orgy of bloodletting to preserve either slavery or the Union. The last year of the war averaged 1,000 deaths a day, and there was doubt that it could last another six months for recruiting and volunteering had so thinned the working population that you could not have both war and agriculture.

Whatever the Confederacy meant to Tiny was now and forever more his secret to keep. One moment Tiny is fiercely alive, laughing, drinking, a man filled with all the rage, lust, sorrow and giddy pleasures a human can know. The next moment, he has joined the fallen legions who will not take up arms again.

Mine was the realization that death is always closer than we think.

I left the bar and walked under the weeping sky with the smell of wet pines and wood smoke in the mist, thinking how sweet life is, and how easily taken for granted.

I should have found a cemetery and laid wreaths on the graves of those who died, for freedom, for flag and country, in honor or in vain. It would have been right to stand in the wet and taste the tears shed on Memorial Day.

Instead I went to the car, waited for the others to arrive from wherever they had gone, and finally drove away. When I turned on the radio, the Beatles were singing "Get Back…"

Radio Daze

IN THE FALL of 1967 I had a job as a radio announcer at a low-powered local AM station that played mostly country western and inoffensive pop music, bracketed by low-budget advertisements for hardware sales and the demolition derby. The station hired me to do the morning "drive time" – which meant turn everything on and get the day rolling with a station ID, the weather report, and then read from the pile of paper beneath the teletype machine that spewed AP wire headlines. They didn't hire me because I was a hotshot DJ, they hired me because I was willing to come in at 6:00 a.m.

There was no engineer – he came in at 8:00 a.m. for the last hour of my shift – so I was pretty much left on my own to play whatever I wanted as long as no one complained, and the commercials got read on the quarter hour. At first it was mostly Herb Alpert and the Tijuana Brass or George Jones on the turntable, but soon enough I slid from what was in the station library into pleasing myself. Why not a little Rolling Stones followed by Coleman Hawkins? How about a blast of Frank Zappa and the Mothers of Invention doing "The Duke of Prunes," paired up with Patsy Kline's "Crazy" or a funky James Brown singing "I'm Black and I'm Proud" as a chaser? I was borrowing records from everyone I knew just to see how many styles of music I could collect. I was playing whatever my mood and the season suggested. I was on the cutting edge of FM before there even was FM. It was Radio Free Winona!

Half the time as I sat with the lights dimmed in that studio I was wondering if we were even on the air. I had reason to wonder as a little note over the control board said, if the needles spike or the board goes dark, throw this switch, (there was a little arrow pointing to a little red toggle switch that was supposed to save the station), announce the call letters as the FCC required when starting transmitting, and ask if we are still on the air, then give the studio number.

That note did nothing to build my confidence in the station's commitment to a state-of-the-art broadcasting technology. Inevitably, the day came when my fears came to pass. I had put The Beatles' "For the Benefit of Mr. Kite" on the turntable and was in the middle of playing the disc when the lights flickered, the needles spiked, and the board went black for a second or two before coming back on line. It was a short pause, but the glitch was enough to spur me into action.

I followed the instructions on the note, flipped the red switch, announced the station call letters, and then got on the microphone and told my listeners if they could hear my transmission to please call the station's phone number. After what seemed like a very long pause I was shocked to hear the phone ring. I picked up the receiver.

Hello?

You're still on the air.

I heard a low voice of indeterminate sex.

Good. Do you listen often?

I wake up to your voice every morning.

My voice?

A smile came to my face with the realization that someone heard me.

She told me her name was Marianne but that was all I learned about her on that first call. It was enough to plant the seed, though. She was listening. In my head I began to plan the morning drive time show around her. What would Marianne like to hear this morning? Over the course of the next month she called a few times to tell me that she liked my playing this or that. I liked the sound of her voice. It got so that around 7 a.m. I'd begin wondering if there would be a call today from my mysterious fan. When she did call, my day was brighter no matter what the weather might be.

I developed a particular mental image of her – her languid body in the bed wearing a sheer black slip... No, better yet, scratch the slip. She was wearing nothing. Yes, I could see the long line of her shapely legs stretching out beneath white sheets, her straight blonde... no, not blonde. She couldn't be a blonde. Her voice was darker, like a slice of German chocolate cake. Better to think of those tresses as raven black. It was total fantasy, but I wanted some image to flesh out the siren song each ring of the phone evoked.

Though I asked leading questions, when she did call, she never talked about herself. Despite my hoping for anything that could fill in the details of where she lived, what she did, or how old she was, my inquiries were batted away. It was like a game, I'd ask and she'd shift the conversation to current events. How the racial tensions after the summer of urban riots seemed to be diminishing. How she thought that the appointment of Thurgood Marshall, as the first African-American Supreme Court justice was a sign of progress. Or she'd discuss the progress of the war she did not support.

Despite my ignorance, or maybe because of it, Marianne engaged me in a lively civic education. At first, I wanted her to answer the questions I had that would move her from imagination closer to my knowing basic facts, but the facts she wanted to share were those of the political and cultural upheaval I was living in post-riot America. At some point I recognized that what she offered in terms of history, politics, and social commentary was as much who she was as the color of her hair.

Then I began looking for the kind of news items she might be interested in. On October 21, tens of thousands of Vietnam War protestors march in Washington, DC while Allen Ginsberg and a band of "happy hippies" surrounded the Pentagon and chanted to symbolically exorcise the war machine of its demons.

Norman Mailer was there, she said. *He's a very good writer. You should read him sometime.*

She suggested other books for me to read – history or philosophy, mostly. It was interesting stuff. More interesting than the assigned texts in my History of Western Civilization class. She said that she had a lot of time to herself, so she read widely. She told me she appreciated it when I'd indulge her conversations about what she was reading

Indulge *her*? By this time, I practically lived to hear her voice. In my head, she was the smart, funny, beautiful woman (who I had never met) who I wanted to date. An absent goddess who's every call made me long to transport myself through the telephone lines and then to materialize next to her on some cloud-obscured Mount Olympus.

But – what then? I wondered; would I be disappointed if the fact of her if she did not match the fantasy?

No, I thought. I would be true to the wit and intelligence of this mystery woman. I decided that when I met her, I would openly embrace whoever she was.

Then one day she called to say that this was good-bye. I was shocked, disappointed, despite myself.

Why?

I'm going to be leaving tomorrow.

My asking her where she was going prompted a long silence.

Somewhere I won't be able to hear you any more, she told me. *But I'll think of you as I travel.*

Then she said, *Play something special for me tomorrow. Some jazz...*

Who? Coltrane? Ellington? Miles Davis?

Yes, Miles, she said.

"Kind of Blue" or new material?

That's a classic. Bill Evans, John Coltrane, Miles...
That'll be the thing to hear before I go.

She hung up the phone.

The next morning in the studio, as I set the needle in the groove I said, *Marianne, this one's for you.* Miles filled the airwaves with his classic meditation on "Blue in Green" and "So What." I turned up the volume, leaned back in my chair, and silently wished her a pleasant journey.

Not quite two weeks later, I sat at my broadcast console, reading the morning paper while I DJed. The November 30th headline said that Minnesota's own senior senator Eugene McCarthy was announcing his candidacy for the nation's highest office, to challenge President Johnson based on the growing opposition to the war. Marianne will be glad to hear that, I thought.

Turning a page, I saw a small article about the police investigating the suspicious death of a 45-year old former college professor suffering from multiple sclerosis. The coroner had deemed it a possible suicide. And there was her name. At least, her familiar first name.

I put on Bach's "Goldberg Variations" and turned on the microphone. What could I say? What should I say? It was too late to change anything but still the words tumbled out.

"I am sitting here in this chair," I said. "In this town called Winona. In the county also called Winona. In a state called Minnesota. In a country called the United States. In the northern half of the western hemisphere. On a planet

called earth. Orbiting a small yellow star we call the sun –
which is itself moving with the outer arm of the Milky Way
galaxy.

"I am here and you, listening for so long, are there. Do
you hear me now? I wanted to say good-bye. No, I wanted to
say hello, to say, thank you for your companionship all these
mornings. And yet, what does it matter now? You are gone."

"I remembered reading somewhere that everything that
we've every broadcast, every electromagnetic wave and bit of
information, every entertainment, every television show,
every radio program, news report, baseball game, all the
broadcast speeches of the notables – Churchill, Hitler,
Kennedy, Martin Luther King – as well as every record –
Chuck Berry, Beethoven, Dylan, Duke Ellington. And yes,
even that broadcast of Miles Davis' 'Kind of Blue' is still
moving outward across the universe. All of it hurtling willy-
nilly into the black void of space."

"Who hears it? Who hears the shouts of joy, the cries for
help? Who receives the exhortations for us to cast the vote,
to pick up the gun, to be here now, to love the one we're with
or to end this slow slide to entropy?"

"I wonder if in some corner of this galaxy or another they
might be listening. Could they be trying to make sense of the
gibberish of this noisy planet? What would that distant
listener think of the jumble spilling across the void of space
and time? What could they possibly think – except that we
swing from love to war and back again, still knowing
nothing, and still trying to do what is right."

Remodeling the Kitchen

MY NEPHEW TOLD ME that when he bought the two-story gray house next to the bakery, it had two problems. The first was the smell of doughnuts every morning drove him crazy. He said he seemed to put weight on day by day, whether he went next door to partake or not. The second problem was that the house was haunted. The realtor had not mentioned that. No one had. He discovered it on his own one night when he went to get a beer before bed.

Entering the darkened kitchen and on his way to the refrigerator, it seemed to him that he was not alone. He turned to see the silhouette of someone, a woman by the look of it, standing by the back-porch door.

Hello. Who's that?

She did not speak but stepped forward into the half-light coming through the window that looked on the bakery's open back door. To his eyes, she looked to be a white woman in her 50's, a thin figure with rounded shoulders wearing a plain dress and gray apron with a pocket on the left side. Her hair, as best he could make it out, was some washed-out shade of brown. He said that everything about her seemed to be like the faded image of a housewife from an old movie. Not transparent, but not fully materialized.

A ghost, he said, *well that's different. What do you want?*

The ghost responded by pointing toward the sink. Following her gesture, he turned, and it suddenly seemed to him the sink was tilted, resting at an odd angle. He hadn't noticed this during the walk through before making the purchase offer on the house. He hadn't thought the sink was off square any of the days he had done dishes there, but now that she pointed it out, he thought he should probably fix it. When he turned back to look at the apparition, he saw nothing. She was gone.

He went to the refrigerator. Opening the door, he wondered if he had imagined seeing the woman. He reached in, retrieved a PBR tall boy and popped the tab. Taking a sip, he looked at the sink a second time. It was tilted, though he had never noticed it before.

Well, he thought, *I'm not imagining a crooked sink.* He shrugged, took another sip of his beer, and left the room.

This appearance was not the only one, just the first. Every visitation had the same pattern. He would come into the kitchen and she would be there in a shadow. Sometimes she stood by the back door and sometimes in the corner by the basement door. She did not speak. Each time the woman appeared she would point to various items: the sink, the floor, the window, and then repeatedly at the refrigerator. Each time he made a note of what she had pointed at and saw some flaw.

Why is she doing this? Why does she appear in the kitchen and nowhere else in the house? And why does she never say anything?

He asked her variations on why and what until her silence was so deeply felt, there was no point in asking.

Try as he might to puzzle it out, he found no rhyme or reason to determine when she appeared. The list he recorded of the ghosts' dissatisfactions grew until the kitchen became unbearably flawed. Like the haunted housewife, everything in the room became in its own way an apparition, like a suggestion of something that should be solid but grew more insubstantial the more he studied it.

My nephew decided that the ghost would not leave until he remodeled the kitchen based on what she had pointed out. He was not sure why she disliked the kitchen but now that she had pointed out the flaws, he didn't like it either.

His wife thought he was taking this haunted kitchen thing too far, but then she had never seen the ghost, not even once. She was sure his plan for remodeling the kitchen was going to cost them more money than they could afford, but by this point, money didn't matter. My nephew said the kitchen had to be redone in hopes the ghost would leave or he would have to sell the house.

He began work. First on the list was to fix the floor, with its old warped boards. When the refrigerator was moved to make way, he saw that the wall behind it had been patched. Curious about what it covered, he took a crowbar to the wall. Inserting the metal tip into a small gap where the plaster and paint leaked dark, he pressed down and with a loud crack the entire patch flew to the floor.

Something wrapped in yellowed newspapers was wedged in place inside the opening. He pulled it out and set it on the floor. The papers were dated April 1928 and as he pulled them away, he saw a metal box. It was a tarnished bronze color about the size of a cigar humidor. Those boxes had been quite popular in that era.

He opened the latch to discover the box was filled with expensive looking jewelry. Diamonds set in necklaces. A small bag of loose cut stones. Fat green emeralds set in a matching broach and bracelet. And all of it was wrapped in a gray kitchen apron.

His first thought was not where this small fortune had come from or why was it there, but that if he sold it there would be enough money to pay for the remodeling.

Thank you, Mrs. Ghost...

His wife did some research to try to find the source of this treasure. Had there been a jewel robbery that year? Or was this cache someone's inheritance hidden away for safekeeping? For all her searching, she found nothing, and they decided to take the pieces a few at a time to appraise and sell to local jewelers. The jewelers were surprised at the quality of the stones and gladly paid top dollar for the lot. My nephew was surprised at how much they got for the ghostly bounty.

As he showed me the new kitchen, with the stainless-steel double sink, refinished floor and all new appliances, I asked about the ghost. Had he seen her lately?

No, he said, he hadn't. But there was one curious thing, he said. After removing the jewelry, he took the grey apron that had protected them in the box and hung it on a hook just behind the basement door. It was there for a day, maybe two, and then it disappeared.

Eve To My Adam

START

AS A CHILD in Albania, she would climb a hundred stairs up the hill to her aunt's house. There might as well have been a thousand for the dread that each one brought. With each step, her fear grew – a fear that once again she would be ordered to stand in the middle of the courtyard. All while her crazed aunt, her suspicious aunt, the aunt of the Evil Eye and unexplained superstitions, curses and charms would whirl a live chicken over her head, and mutter words she did not understand, as if words alone were enough to re-make the world.

Amid the squawking and flapping of wings, the old woman chanted hexes and prayers, blending exhortation and pleadings in three languages, all to drive away the demons and spirits she was certain possessed the child. Then the exorcism would culminate with the old woman cutting the chicken's head off and sprinkling the blood in the child's face.

Be gone Lilith. Let blood appease your hunger.

Her father told her it was just an old woman's joke, but the sight of the stairs drove her to tears. Rooted in the stony ground of fear she would have to be dragged to the upper floor, eyes closed, wishing that she were somewhere else.

START AGAIN

WE HAD AN AFFAIR. Or, rather, we almost had an affair. Or perhaps we pretended we weren't having one, even when we behaved like we were having one. In any case, since she wished to remain technically faithful to her absent husband, the thought of an actual affair was as terrifying as the climb up the stairs of her childhood. So we substituted booze and ontology for sex.

I seduced her in a kitchen with a fine single malt from a bottle that she could never afford on a graduate teaching assistant's salary. She didn't drink scotch or any hard liquor before we met. She didn't like the taste or smell of it, but in the late and smoky hours as a party wore down, when the music was turned up and small talk turned boring and the black hole of the kitchen pulled everything to its core, she polished off three shots – no ice, no mix – like it was the nectar of *amoré*.

Sitting on my lap, she laughed, put her arms around me and kissed me. It was a kiss that had no history or precedent. It was not a chaste little kiss, or a sloppy alcohol nuzzle, but intentional; of the moment, for the moment, and very much in the moment. Surprising in its passion, it spoke of a desire that I would savor and parse for months afterward. It was the kind of kiss that gave a man notions. Once I had them, I was tormented by Could, Would and Should. I admonished her.

Don't open any doors you are not prepared to walk through.

You know me.

Not really. Not in the ways that count.

She laid her head on my shoulder and said softly,

Then we shall have to change that.

Picking up the bottle, I took a sip.

I propose that we show each other the shadow, the monster hiding under the bed, the essential body naked and unashamed.

The thought of you seeing me like that frightens me.

She waved the bottle away.

The thought of not knowing who is on my lap, who is whispering in my ear... What do you want, Eve? To tease me, to play at offering the apple to my Adam?

She put her finger to my lips, got off my lap, pulled me to my feet and opened the door.

You should go now.

MIDDLE

WHEN SHE WAS TEN, her family moved across the closed border for reasons that were vague to her. They went to Paris and then to New York. In both cities they lived in cheap hotels. In the former she spent long hours looking out the window at the barges traveling the Seine. In the latter, she looked past the alley with the honk of horns and the clang and clatter of the garbage trucks taking away America's excess and toward the high rises glistening in a starless night sky. In the former they ate flaky crusted baguettes with soft cheeses at small tables. In the latter, mice lived in the drawers and nibbled the chocolate bars she kept hidden under the socks.

America became not a land of opportunity, but rather a land of unseen scurrying and diminishing pleasures.

INDETERMINATE

MONTHS PASSED as she and I flirted in small kitchens; mostly hers, but sometimes it would be in other faculty member's homes, where our standing that close was ignored. Ours was a romance marked by awkward questions, hesitant answers, the offering and the rejecting of philosophical definitions, suggestions of writers we should read who spoke of the subject at hand better than we could. Then the tenor changed. Poems we found with the right sense of danger or romance gave way to poems we wrote and immediately tore into pieces when they were read.

Sometimes we danced.

The husband, who was not there and not coming home, was neither asked nor spoken about. He might as well have been dead, but every once in a while, I would see evidence of his still being in the world. Letters lying open on the table and once, a paisley tie hanging on the back of a chair.

Our passion was played out as we danced between Formica tables and sinks filled with dishes waiting for baptism. Holding my hands like a child clutching her father's, she would lean back, eyes closed, her throat a long graceful curve of flesh, and ask to be twirled in a circle.

I would begin a slow counter clockwise movement as she leaned further out.

Stop that. It's too much.

You're the one who asked for this.

How can you be standing there, the room is moving, the lights spin and the whole world is dizzy? Everything is in motion.

You're making it move, Eve. Perception quantifies experience. It begins with your desire and goes out from there.

Then I must be beyond dizzy, delightfully mad. No, you are the one who is mad. You are contagious. You bring out the madness in people, in me. What am I doing here with you? I knew my purpose before I met you.

I claim no madness but my own. I accept it in myself, in others, as the way of all flesh.

Reeling her in I could feel her animal heat beneath the white silk blouse, the wild beating of her heart as I held her close.

You are such a temptation. Well named, Eve, Adam's helpmate wanting to taste of the fruit of the Tree of Life.

You are the serpent.

I said to her, *You say that to dismiss your desire.*

She reached out for another scotch and poured it into her open mouth. A trickle ran down her cheek, down her neck, into her cleavage. She licked her lips.

Desire makes us strong. It drives us to accomplish what otherwise would be inconvenient.

No, dear, I have been watching you all these months and I know that you don't desire me, not really, not my body, not even my tenderness. You want something that cannot be possessed. You believe in consequences but never want to taste the regret of choices. You believe in faithfulness but want the freedom of forgiveness. But I know as you should that there can be no forgiveness without sin. For that you have to take the apple.

She leaned against me, put her finger to my lips cautioning me to not say another word. Running that long finger over my forehead, through my hair, she whispered in my ear.

Pour me my temptation...

When she passed out, I carried her to the bedroom. I laid her on the bed, took off her shoes. Only that. She might want to taste the fruit of the tree and forget if she could not be forgiven. But even if I could be forgiven, I would not forget.

FINISH

NEAR THE END we met in a small cafe. She was leaving to join her husband in Israel.

You're a Catholic, or used to be one. You used to be a priest, didn't you?

Yes, I was once. Recovering now.

Well Priest, I want to make a confession. Do you know that to be a Jew is to be born in a heritage of separateness? God's chosen people. I cannot forget my separateness, or even really disguise it. I might as well wear a yellow star. I'm an exile from the world of family and marriage. She stopped and looked at her hands. *I feel like an exile from the God of my people, from that first Garden where we could be innocent, from myself.*

Eve picked up her coffee then put it back down again.

My body is a traitor, my mind a succubus. Call me Lilith. It's the spirit that my aunt knew as my true name, the one I should have taken.

I looked up from the cup of lukewarm latte to study her November dark hair and the eyes made for longing. I watched every breath trembling at the door of her sensual mouth, the pale hands with the long fingers so well suited to the piano. I had heard her play once, but when I asked her about it, she said she had no talent. Everything was confusion. If she could commit to something between us, I would without regret, but since she would not, I couldn't.

She turned in her chair, took my hand in hers. *And yet it takes an act of will to remain different.*

I kissed her hand. *I have always thought that to believe, to live by faith is to set oneself on a particular path, and though you turn aside or leave it, those departures determine the quality of our experience but not the world we are taught to see. We begin childhood by naming the world and then we live in it. For better or worse, we know only what we know. Although I am also an exile, I became a nomad while I was still a child. I've spent my life traveling from one crowded souk and welcome oasis to another, always knowing the root and soil I sprang from.*

I traveled as a child...

She pouted, her face trying hard not to betray the realization and disappointment that she had never thought of herself as a nomad.

She believed in the wrathful God after the Garden, the God who posted angels with flaming swords between our selves and any kind of happiness. The fickle God of Moses, the deliverer of hardship and exile, the giver of stone tablets. Yet in that belief she longed for the surety of a column of smoke by day and a pillar of fire by night, for the generous God of manna in a desert landscape. She longed for something different at the top of the stairs that would make it worth climbing the hundred steps.

I wanted to exorcise the memory of the blood-splattering aunt of those hundred stairs for her. To say your exile is over; here, rest in the cool of my tent. I wanted to banish the ghost of a religion that haunted her with its emptiness. Neither belief nor doubt offered a path or comfort.

Who was I to think such thoughts? Even if I had freed myself from my own faith, I believed in nothing but stories of wanderers, or perhaps, if I was truthful, in a search for a temple worth entering or an altar worthy of sacrifice. The most I could offer her was to not be alone in the desert, but this would not be enough. One of us was always moving towards, and the other away from, the promised land of milk and honey.

We looked across the table knowing that our suitcases had been packed from the first night we had seen each other. In our silence we held each other's hands as tenderly as fireflies caressing twilight in a clover field and though we were here, we had already departed.

Barbeque Bus

OUT OF A MOONLESS NIGHT, two black buses roared along the winding state highway.

With the first sliver of day they pulled into the Wal-Mart parking lot at the edge of a comfortably sleeping town that was like any town or every town you know. Black from end to end, not a stitch of chrome, windows of dark tinted glass, no markings to say who or where they came from, engines idling like a two-pack smoker's dying breath, they shimmered like obsidian in the deserted parking lot – a question waiting to be asked.

With the rising of the welcome crimson sun, the doors opened and from the inside came four enormous black men with shaved heads and bare oiled chests. They took four immense grills from the luggage bays, each wide enough to lay a man on top. They must have poured bag after bag of black lump charcoal into those long troughs, although it seemed they poured but one bag each, and when they fired up those mighty kettles, columns of smoke and flame leapt to the heavens like pillars of sacrifice.

Precisely at seven, they raked the coals and began to lay upon the grills the day's votive offerings: pork ribs and baby backs on one, quartered chicken on another, beef brisket and short ribs on the third and on the fourth, something undetermined. Although meat it most definitely was, from what animal or what quarter was anybody's guess.

At each glowing kettle, the shining demigods of the grill stood with tongs or brushes at the ready. From inside the other bus, a shadowy figure moved about, more sensed than seen, periodically giving orders over loudspeakers in a low voice whose commands set the four silent and glistening men to turn this or baste that with a vinegary red sauce.

The smoke and smell of searing flesh crept through the streets and alleys like a lost cat, scratching at every door, testing each window and crack for a welcome. Soon the odor found entrance and as sure as day follows night, the sleepers rose from their beds. Whether awake or still dreaming I will not say, but entranced and casting modesty aside, they came out of their houses. Some came naked and some in their 'jammies, like so many sleepwalkers drawn to the source of their desire, moving, steadily moving, toward the empty parking lot and the keepers of the burning coals.

Not a single word was spoken while the milling crowd organized itself into a line trailing from one end of the asphalt to the other, each patiently waiting to receive, in his or her turn, a paper plate which they held before them like shameless alms seekers. No money was requested, and no payment was offered. One by one the unconscious townsfolk stepped to the grills to have their culinary fate decided by the all-seeing, unseen presence who portioned out their rations with a single command of "Pig," "Bird," "Cow," or "Gift." They took the offerings with unseeing eyes. They did not ask but did receive the glistening dollops of fiery sauce that followed without smile or frown, without an uttered please or thank-you. Utensils, napkins – these were not offered, nor were they needed.

Surely it was half the town, or perhaps all the town, standing there or fallen to the ground as true carnivores must, tearing away great chucks of the seared flesh with hungry mouths. They knew no shame, but fell on the warm meat like wolves, fighting for scraps, collapsing into fetal posture as they gnawed the gristle and sucked bone marrow.

A few tried to get back into line, but the stains of the ambrosial sauce marked them and they were turned away with snapping tongs to weep inconsolably. Just when all hope of satisfaction was lost, the commanding voice offered a reprieve:

You may have more... of the Gift.

And they began to line up again to receive the only meat left on any of the grills. As much as was put on the plate, the supply seemed inexhaustible, always full no matter how many came, and yet for those with plates in hand the portions were never quite enough to satisfy.

The afternoon clock struck six. In an instant the grills were empty, the four shadows of men pouring the white-coated coals in a smoking circle around the buses. A curtain of shimmering smoke obscuring the view and along the asphalt edge the red glow of the fire beneath the ashes shone all about as the sound of the grills loaded back into the luggage bays was heard. The doors hissed shut and at that very moment the townspeople awoke to their shame – naked, semi-naked, clothed with grease stains, standing in piles of discarded plates amid piles of clean picked bone. The black apparition's engines roared to life. The buses seemed not so much to drive through the ring of smoking coals but right into them, and then they were gone.

It was only then that the hunger truly came upon them. A hunger that could not be satisfied and would not go away. As tragic a tune for bitter Fate as any Greek chorus, a song began with someone and moved like a virus through the crowd until they were all singing.

Now Ken and Barbie know their fate

Looking at the sauce-stained plate

They'll never see Paradise again

Now that they've tasted bone.

Big ribs, real ribs, smoky ribs,

   from the King of Barbeque

I say, BIG ribs, reeeaal ribs, smooookey ribs,

A Gift heaped upon the plate,

   from the King of Barbeque...

Wooing Constance

I was giving Larry, an under-employed anthropologist, a ride to the wedding of a mutual friend. He did not look particularly academic but rather had a kind of loose-limbed athleticism that was, as he said, suited for rugby. He was a talker though, slipping from one topic to another by way of a long set of digressions. I wasn't paying much attention until I heard this story:

WHEN I WAS a grad student at the University of Chicago, I began to date Constance who was everything other than Midwestern. She was Scottish, with red hair and a mercurial disposition and a lilting accent that I found both charming and disarming. We got on well. At the end of the term she told me that she was going to return home. Naturally I was disappointed that I would not be able to keep wooing her.

A few weeks after the semester ended, Constance was gone, and I realized that I was in love with her. So much so that I thought we should marry. You'd think it was rash decision based on one semester of dating, but really, how often would I have the opportunity to meet a girl like that again?

I decided to surprise her with a visit and a ring. The ring cost me half the money I had saved for next semester's tuition and the plane ticket to London was going to cost me close to half of what was left. It would be worth the price. I flew to London, took the train to Edinburgh, and then a bus to the small town where Constance told me she lived.

When I asked him the name of the town, he replied, It doesn't matter. What matters is what followed.

There wasn't much to the town. A gaggle of two-story buildings mostly made of brick with pastel trim. A white-washed church on a hill with a surprisingly large cemetery stretching from the building to the road below; across the only paved road, a few stores leaned towards each other, one garage at the edge of town with a single gas – or as they call it, "petrol" – pump in front. Not much to the place to entertain a visitor except for the local pub called the Black Dog. When I asked about accommodations, I was told the Black Dog doubled as an inn. It was there I went to get a room and the directions to her house.

The bar man who was also the innkeeper was also, he told me, the postmaster. He was friendly enough. I couldn't really tell whether it was his natural disposition or just a face he wore for a visitor. A short man, ruddy complexion, he huffed with every breath as though it would be his last. His stomach was the very definition of beer belly. He was happy to give me a room if I didn't mind a shared bath. I'd lived in college dorms long enough to not care and said so.

"Top of the stairs, second door on the right, if it please you."

"What about a key?" I asked.

"We've no need of that here, sir, but the door will lock on the inside if you don't wish to be disturbed."

I asked him for the directions to Constance's house and his beaming smile faltered.

"Going to see the Laird are you?"

"No, going to see his daughter."

"He has no daughter."

"I'm going to see Constance. I went to school with her in the States. In Chicago."

"Oh, then that makes it all the more clearer. You mean Constance, the niece."

"Niece?"

"Yes, Constance and her sister, Faith. They're the Laird's wards. Tragic it was, the accident that took his brother and left them two girls orphans. But family being what they are, he's raised them up as if they were his own."

"All well and good," I said, "but if you will, how do I get there?

"By car or bike or your own two feet?

"Does it make a difference – never mind – by my own two feet."

"Here then," he said. "If you'll be walking, I'll make you a wee map on this napkin." He wrote down a set of directions that largely consisted of looking for landmarks that were not there – 'Turn on the lane where the old school stood,' that sort of thing. To his credit though, he was sparing in what went on the napkin. By the time he finished his narrative, I had a general sense of how to walk the two or so miles to the Laird's manor.

It was a pleasant walk out of town, and I did indeed follow the small lane next to the stone foundation of what was probably the old school house. The lane wound through one of the few old woods left in this part of the country. Rounding a bend, I saw a large three-story house. I suppose you'd call it stately, in that English manor house style, with two wings facing each other across a courtyard, and lots of brick and timbered accents.

I figured that there was no point in hesitating; I went up and knocked on the door. A woman who resembled Constance opened the door. She was younger and much thinner. I guessed it to be her sister, Faith.

"Who are you?"

"I'm Larry, your sister's boyfriend. Is Constance home?"

"The American boyfriend!" She laughed. "Well I never expected to see you. Please do come in. Oh, this will be grand."

For her, I suppose it was grand. I realized that if she never expected to see me, then Constance didn't expect to see me either. Not there and then. She was sitting in a large room. I suppose you would call it a parlor, or maybe a drawing room. It certainly was not a living room though – it was too formal for that. Portraits of pale old men staring out of dark backgrounds hung on walls painted a deep green. There was an ornate and rather uncomfortable looking couch no one was sitting in, and several matching chairs that were occupied.

"Larry, this is a surprise."

She rose from her chair, turned towards me, then turned back toward the two men sitting in the other chairs. One man was older, with a thick thatch of wheat colored hair, wearing an expensive suit. The other was about my age, not exactly handsome, but close enough to good looking in that way men who can afford to take care of themselves look. He had the build of an athlete. Not Rugby, but maybe soccer or rowing.

From the way she moved toward me, hesitated and then backed away, I thought she was embarrassed to kiss me in front of them.

"Larry," she said, "this is my uncle John, and this is my fiancé John."

Now it was my turn to be confused and embarrassed. How could she be engaged to another man while I came all this way with a ring in my pocket? A ring with only one purpose, and now that purpose was mocked. I felt a fool. I should have told her I wanted to marry her while she was still in Chicago.

Fiancé John looked to be upset at my arrival. Maybe he could sense my intent. Pheromones or something that immediately makes him start alpha dog posturing. He began with a taunt, suggesting that I was an uncultured American. I retorted that for a tight assed Englishman, he was showing his prejudices. "Historically inbred as you people are," I continued, "perhaps as you were able to subjugate the Scots and Irish, but we colonists slipped the noose."

Constance coughed. Faith asked if I would be staying in the house. The uncle coughed. The younger sister laughed and left the room.

I said, "I'd like to talk to you, Constance."

"Not now, Larry. Not today. Oh dear, my schedule is full for tomorrow, so if you would be a dear, come by the next day and we'll have a proper tea." She leaned over to give me a peck on the cheek and pushed me towards the door at the same time.

I could take a hint and left. The last thing I heard before the door shut was, the sister, saying, "Oh, please, DO come back again!"

All the way back to the village I tried to replay every bit of the rom-com of Constance in Chicago – every flirtation, every Windy City date, every time we kissed, the days we woke up in the same bed. There was a lot there to review and as my mood darkened, I wanted to sulk with a pint in hand.

I was into my third glass at the Black Dog when Fiancé John arrived, intent on one more round of insulting the American. Fuck him. I let him get three taunts out, counting each one on my fingers, before the fingers folded themselves into a fist and caught him on his still open jaw. He staggered back, shaking his head, and then charged at me. At the last possible moment, I slid to the right letting him crash into the bar. One of the locals whistled his appreciation. I was still holding my half-full pint, which I put down on a table and turned to face John. He came towards me a second time but instead of stepping back or aside, I lunged at him, chest bumping him like we were crowing cocks fighting for mating rights.

Which I suppose we were. The barkeep shouted and other patrons, three or four to a man, separated us.

"What's your deal?" I said, "What gives you any more right to Constance than I have?"

"Family ties, money, culture," he replied. "Just because the lass goes to America on a lark, it does not make her fair game for poaching. She was mine before she left and she's mine now that she's returned."

"Bullshit. But if you want her, we can stand here beating the crap out of each other until one of us is left. I'm pretty sure that in spite of your size and obvious muscle tone, it would still be me. After all, we uncouth Americans know a thing or two about kicking British ass."

He charged me again, only to be held back. Someone suggested that we have a foot race to settle this. A quick jaunt across the moor where the winner would get to court the girl and the loser would leave. Fiancé John says we should race at twilight and the collective gasp that followed told me that everyone in the room thinks it's a terrible idea.

Day or night or in between, I can take this pouty prick. So I agreed and said, "You can set out the course."

Fiancé John says, "A 5K loop that goes out and back, crossing the Tornhead Bridge and ending at this very spot." There is another louder collective gasp, and someone says that crossing the bridge is a terrible idea, that it is not safe even in daylight.

Fiancé John laughs, and since I don't know shit about some bridge, I don't say anything. There's a moment's pause as the room waits for whatever is coming next. I say, "You're so on – we'll run the course tomorrow evening," and go back to drinking my waiting pint.

In the morning the barkeep has a kid who looks to have as many pimples as freckles walk me over the course. It was mostly out the door, up the hill, down, across the heather strewn fields in a long loop and then up another hill and down to where the bridge stood. The kid got a little nervous as we approached the bridge.

"Something wrong?" I asked.

"Well, the story goes that it's haunted. I can't say that I've ever had any fact of it, but I will tell you what every mother I've ever heard says. When you arrive at the bridge do not stop or look back no matter what happens. Do you hear me, man? You set one foot on the bridge, like we are about to do, and you run as fast as you can to the other end."

And with that the kid takes off like his life depended on it. I figured it was some kind of old wives' tale, but I did the same, and ran as fast as I could across the span. Nothing happened, and I figured it was just some kind of local scare to keep kids from playing on the bridge.

As evening approached the pub filled with the curious and the betting kind. Odds are on the fiancé as he is from this side of the pond but a few of them think an American is capable. Either way, there hasn't been anything going on this interesting in the town for a long time. A girl who looks to be in high school wishes me well, and tells me that if I lose I can court her.

Constance and her sister are nowhere in sight. Whether they even know about this is subject to speculation, but I don't have time for it now. My future and my stamina are about to be tested.

A ceremonial glass of whiskey was offered and each of us downed it to cheers. A second was poured for the winner and placed on a shelf next to the bar. The first man to reach it and sip at the end of the run would be declared the winner.

The door was opened, and that precocious high school girl stood, and waved a red handkerchief. We bolted through the door, turned right towards the edge of town and headed out to open countryside.

I didn't know how well the fiancé knew the course, but my strategy was to let him take the lead, while I remained a few steps behind as we went over the rise and into the moor. I was sure that I'd know the right moment to pass him and once I did pass, I'd double my pace.

At first it seemed simple enough. The sun was not quite to the horizon, the hillsides were bathed in warm yellow. But where the shadows fell, it took on a strange, pinkish-gray tone which reminded me of the old saying that twilight was the favored time between the Worlds when humans were at risk of becoming bewitched by fairies.

A thin mist was rising in the low places and it became harder to follow Fiancé John. There was a moment when the cloud was up to my knees that I slipped on a wet patch and fell. Getting to my feet, there was no time to brush away mud and matted leaves as I could see he was stepping into the rapidly thickening fog in a low spot. If I was to keep him in sight, I needed to redouble my effort now.

In a minute I was close enough to hear his footsteps ahead of me, even if I couldn't see him. The way our strides sounded he heard mine getting closer as well, and he picked up his pace. I could barely recognize the trail. As much as I wanted to slow down for fear of tripping again, I focused entirely on the rhythm of John's feet hitting the ground as he ran. Suddenly, the trail rose and we were out of the fog. I had to pass him just as we came to the top. As I came up behind him to pull ahead, he gave me a shove, but I was expecting it, and I stepped aside. Off balance, he stumbled. I reached back to push him off the course, and I heard him land heavy in the heather. I did not look back but plunged onward, knowing the bridge was just ahead.

When I came to the bottom of the hill, I could barely see the stone edge of the bridge in the thick gloom, but reached out, intent on running my fingers along it as I crossed the span.

Suddenly something leapt on my back. My first thought is that it was the fiancé, my rival. But then I realized it couldn't be John – the weight on my shoulders and back was tremendous, much heavier than a man. Whatever it was, its bulk drove me to my knees, with a rough, guttural breath and a stench like rotting wood. A tremendous cold invaded my body from the center of that weight. It felt as if I was being choked even though I couldn't see anything reaching around my throat. My breath caught, my lungs unable to fill, and I felt I'd do anything to stop that vice grip of pain and damp cold driving my knees to the ground.

I wanted to look back, but I remembered what the kid told me. All my focus was on forward movement, to crawl if I had to, to reach the far end. Then, I don't know why the thought came to me, or the strength to even say the words. With what little voice I had left I called out.

"Take the one who comes after me."

I heard Fiancé John stepping on the bridge, and as quickly as it had come the weight and the cold suffocating my body was gone. The relief was intense and immediate, but I did not stop to think. I lunged forward.

There was a strangled cry behind me in the fog. I didn't turn to look. Feeling lighter, I got to my feet and ran again, not caring if I was even on the trail. Every step took me away from the bridge. The town was less than a kilometer ahead. Splashing, slipping, falling to ground and rising again, I continued through the dankness until I could see the lights of the village before me.

I made it to the pub and burst through the Black Dog's door. There were cheers and groans. The barman handed me the whiskey. I downed the shot in a single swallow and began coughing. He poured me another and told me to sip it this time, but I was not interested in the glass. I tried to tell them what happened, but the barkeep put his finger to his lips and shook his head.

"Not now, lad, we've all heard that story. He'll be along in a minute."

We all waited, but Fiancé John never came through the door.

I drank as many whiskeys as were put in front of me and at some point, someone walked me to my room. Maybe it was the high school girl, for she was in my bed when I woke in the morning.

I was in terrible pain and embarrassed to see her there. I got up, dressed and left the room. Downstairs the innkeeper smiled at me and said, "Well, you've made quite a name for yourself in this town."

"Fuck that," I said, "What happened to him?"

"Ahhh, yes, well we'll be organizing a search party to go out looking for the lad, but I don't have much hope we'll find anything."

He was right. Fiancé John was not found.

I ask Larry is that true? He was never found or heard from again?

I'll tell you what is true, Constance was pissed; she asked how I could be so foolish, but my answer didn't matter to her. She continued, demanding to know why I had never thought to ask her what she wanted before I fucked around with Fiancé John. Why hadn't I told her about the stupid race? She said that I had proved myself to be unworthy – exactly what Fiancé John had called me – a boorish, callous and careless American. She slapped me and told me to go away.

I knew there would be no fixing this one. She was done and I might as well take my ring and go home. Maybe I could sell it in London and take a few days in a decent hotel to get my head together.

Sensing the story had come to an end, I asked him, was there any explanation for what happened on the bridge?

None. In that village no one wanted to hear about it and everywhere else, no one believes it, he said.

We drove in silence for a while, the landscape of central Wisconsin flowing past the windshield, one bog and stand of pines after another. I was thinking about the story. Not about the facts of it but about what I would have done if it had been me.

Out of nowhere Larry says, adventure or misadventure, when you're young it's all the same.

Then

1.) I've been called the Devil in Tennessee.

1a.) 8 AM. I'm sitting on the curb outside a Bristol hotel smoking a decent cigar after a long night of drinking, poker, and lies. Left both of them, the blonde and the dark one, sleeping in the bed. They were fun girls, ready for whatever, and I was the one to bring out the shameless in them. In the wee hours they were as interested in each other's charms as they were in mine and I was happy to sit watching while they rolled and tumbled to joy.

Yes, I went out for my morning constitutional. Went out to watch the sun rise over the fine blue mist of the Smoky Mountains.

A group of bible-thumping Evangelicals are coming out of the hotel – clean-shaven, bright eyed and bushy tailed, wearing their starched white shirts and skinny black ties, well-worn Bibles in hand – on their way to Sunday services. They took one look at me, think to themselves: "Oh my God, it's the Devil."

Taking a long pull on the Cuban, savoring it, I say to no one in particular: "That's right, you run to church now and pray. This is Sunday, everyone's day of rest, even mine. Tomorrow I go back to work just like the rest of you."

2.) Stopped to gas up the classic fog gray Jaguar outside of Madison, Wisconsin and when I turned on to the entrance ramp to the freeway I saw him. Hitchhiking. Looked an awful familiar, like some fellow I knew. Couldn't quite place the name but it would come to me.

Long hair, ragged beard, dressed in worn slacks and a faded white shirt under a stained raincoat. Looked like any fellow that needed a helping hand. I can do that. So I rolled down the window and said, "Get in."

Once he sat down, I realized it was a mistake. Maybe I didn't know this guy but sure knew the smell of sulfur and sweat. I was thinking I'd just leave the window open for a while to air it out, but soon gave up on that idea. It wasn't going to air out till he left.

2a.) "Where you going?" I asked.

"Minneapolis or maybe St. Paul."

"All the way to Minneapolis?"

"Me too."

"Yah, that's what you just said."

How far he might really be going or how long I would let him stay in the car was a question I had not answered yet.

2b.) "This is a mighty fancy car."

"Yes, the fruits of my Herculean labors."

"Are you an apple farmer?"

"No, I'm... Never mind. What I do is what I do."

3.) I ask him: "What did you say your name was?"

"Bob."

"Bob. That's a palindrome."

"Is that your name? Pal 'n' something?"

"No, I haven't said my name. Your name – Bob – is a palindrome, a word that's the same backwards or forwards. Like 'Madam I'm Adam,' or 'Bob.'"

"B-O-B," He spelled it out. "B-O-B. You're right; it is."

4.) 2 PM. I was at the Burger King getting something. Didn't matter much what it was 'cause it all tasted the same to me. What interested me was the girl at the counter. Young thing wearing her shirt loosely buttoned as if to suggest more cleavage than she actually had. Unhappiness was written all over her face. Didn't like the job, the boyfriend, her high school, or the town she was living in. She'd do anything for something different, so I asked her straight out, "Would you sell your soul for a better life?"

She laughed. "No one talks like that. You shouldn't say those kinds of things."

I laughed, "Sorry to have offended. You don't look like a good church girl to me, but the question remains."

She didn't say yes, so much as just put her finger to her lips in a "don't say it" gesture that turned to a smile.

I pulled a Polaroid camera out of my bag and snapped her picture. I pulled a Sharpie out of my suit coat pocket and offered it to her. "In the old days there was some muss or fuss with blood, but no more. Just sign your name and the world will be your oyster. If you believe, I cannot deceive."

She looks at me cross-eyed but takes the pen and makes her mark.

I put the picture in the bag with the camera and the pen and turn back to smile at her. She's thinking it's a joke, but in a week, she'll be rid of the boyfriend. In a month, she'll come into more money than she has ever seen and this town will be so gone.

After that, it will be...

well...

The cliché is: *it will be what it will be.*

I knew what it would be, even if she didn't.

5.) Late that same day, or the night following the day, I was driving a rented Pontiac through the dark Kentucky hills on some twisty two-lane highway, playing radio roulette. Every Gospel, bluegrass and heavy metal station had twenty seconds to hold my attention. Tales of cheating lovers, of money for nothing, and cheap time slot preachers filled the band width with exhortations to repentance, the plinking of furious banjos, the praising of the Lord. It made no difference what was received since it was all static and distortion, here and gone with the next turn.

The car cornered like a bad drunk, brakes squealed like a frightened pig every single time I stepped on them. The speedometer winked at seventy-five, eighty as I plunged into a dark valley with the half-watt lights of some neglected town at the bottom.

This car is pure Detroit junk, but the dashboard light glow is coal-fire red.

Familiar and comforting, it was.

I've got the blonde with good tits on the seat next to me, her head in my lap, wanting to confess her past indiscretions, and the skinny dark haired one in back whispering in my ear, "...faster, Baby Cakes, faster..."

6.) "Do you mind if I take my medicine?"

"Be my guest."

So He-Of-The-Pungent-Odor unzips the small brown bag on his lap, pulls out four bottles of different pills, and looks at one, then another, like he's never seen them before. Inside the bag there's something furry moving around. Creeps me out and I don't scare easy.

"Say, could you zip that bag up?" He looks at me sideways, shrugs, takes one pill from each container, and chews them noisily as he shoves everything including the furry whatever back into the bag and zips it.

6a.) "Can we listen to the radio?"

"I'd rather not. There isn't much on except religion and country music. Not that I've got anything against either of them in their place."

"What place is that?"

"Not in this car."

7.) "How long have you been hitching rides?"

"Since '72 when I was up in Alaska and..."

"Really? I was in Alaska myself about then."

7a.) "It was a misspent youth. Did some of this and that with a good-time Charlie...."

"Was that his name?"

"Damn, you'd think you could remember something like that."

Yes, given how much time was spent with What's-His-Name and the girl, a real pretty dark-eyed girl, you'd think I would remember. A real spitfire she was. The three of us smoking quite a bit o' the wacky weed and drinking sun up to sun down. It was summer. There was a lot of day between sun up and sun down.

7b.) "If I'd met you then, I probably wouldn't remember your name."

"Maybe not, Bob, but you should try."

8.) Then it all came back into focus. That day. The three of us in a fake wood-sided Ford station wagon. We were totally in the cups. We're weaving up the logging road with her giving me a blowjob in the back seat. Like I said – a real willing-to-try-anything girl.

Over the crest of the hill comes a big rig, a red Peterbilt with lots of chrome, full up with hundred-year wood. I can hear the driver downshift; see the billow of smoke from the diesel.

Then there's nothing but an awful silence. Everything slow and inevitable, as the chain snaps the link; the log, six-foot-wide, slides out of the stack like a switchblade, floating into space as the rig bounces down the line.

8a.) Nothing stops.

8b.) I've dreamt it over and over. The truck starts to pass, and the log caves the windshield in with me looking at the old tree rings. Rough bark against flesh, the tearing of metal and the screech of brakes. When it was over I wasn't dead, so I just crawled out and walked away. Why look back?

9.) Yes, I've been called the Devil in Tennessee.

Do you really believe it's easier to get forgiveness than permission? Heard that one before? That if there is no sin, there can be no redemption?

You've always had my permission. I know what all men desire, to sin and to be forgiven. For a small price I offer both.

9a.) Cast your mind back, back, to the secret places, to the memories of what you said and did that should never see the light of day. I know what's in the troubled heart and will ease it. I can offer solace if that's what you think will clean the slate. It won't, but false hope is better than no hope at all.

9b.) I might have thought those sentiments, but I wouldn't say them out loud. Just like I won't say my name 'cause it has power. If it shimmers in the air, and is caught...

Words bind and the will of He That Speaks Them must be done.

10.) "Do you know me?"

"Should I?"

"Think again."

"I swear you look familiar. I forget. It's been a long time."

10a.) I'm the bad dream you cannot wake from, the shadow that will not stay on the wall. I'm the one traveling the highways from the very moment you turned your back on suffering. The one who knew that if you lived, we would meet again. The one I've searched for.

11.) "Say it."

"B-O-B."

"Yes, pleased to meet you."

Tongue of Angels

IN A FAR COUNTRY, in a time now so long ago it can barely be remembered or mercifully forgotten, the house of Dr. Natal was filled with books. Books of every size and topic, shelf after shelf of leather-bound ancient tomes lined the walls and gave the rooms the smell of comfortable antiquity. In that time, many people in that country could not read and even fewer owned books, so the doctor's collection was both a source of wonder and a true national treasure. Many scholars and priests, politicians and businessmen journeyed from the far corners of the land to read those wonderful words containing all manner of wisdom, folly, superstition, rumor, science and belief.

One day Dr. Natal announced to all present that he was leaving on a journey and had entrusted the care of his house and his books to his neighbor, Bocello. Every ear heard his words and every head those ears hung on shook in disbelief.

Bocello was what you might call a simple man, uneducated, unable to read a word. The only book Bocello knew was the Bible, which he sat with for hours at a time, looking at the many beautiful illustrations that inspired him to imagine each of the stories of faith that were shown. Some people thought it strange that such a treasure would be left in the care of one who could not make use of it, but it was agreed that it was Dr. Natal's house, and it was his decision, and it was probably just a temporary measure as he was expected to return soon.

The weeks passed, then months, and as the months stretched into years, the good Doctor did not return. All the while Bocello faithfully tended the collection, dusting the books, putting each back in its proper place when visitors took one down to study its contents, though in truth there was a dwindling frequency of visitors. Many who had come in the day did so as much for Natal's conversation as for any literary tome they might study in the half-shadowed comfort of the great rooms.

Then war broke out in some other place, spread and intensified until like a plague it arrived at that city's gates in the form of an unyielding, largely unseen, enemy. A terrible siege began and went on for weeks that eventually turned to months, and the months threatening to stretch into years. With every false hope and rumor that relief was at hand, things only got worse. There was no movement in or out of the city. No help arrived, and the population learned the meaning of want. No medicine. No food.

The people took to eating rats until there were no rats, and when those were gone, they ate grass and the roots of the wild flowers that managed to grow despite the constant shelling.

When winter came, there was no heat. Bocello was forced to burn the furniture to keep warm. The tables, the chairs, and finally the bookshelves themselves went into the fire. Bocello carefully removed books from each shelf and stacked them in piles along the walls as insulation as he went.

It got colder and stayed so bitterly cold for such a long time that when Bocello left the one room where the tiny fire resided, his bones shook as if to break. Fingers and toes went numb and forgotten until the pain was such, he thought they would fall off. Then the day came when all the bookshelves were gone and Bocello was left with nothing to burn but the books or the clothes on his back.

He could not betray Dr. Natal's trust, and so, he lay down beside the weakened flame to sleep a last, long sleep. In a dream, Dr. Natal stood before him, sweeping his hand over the piles of books and said, "Books are good, but people are better, Bocello. Burn the books for their knowledge resides in the many that have read them."

Bocello awoke and with tears in his eyes began to reluctantly feed the books, one at a time, into the fire. As he did so, there was a most curious result. Each book seemed to burn slower and cast more heat than the last, but even stranger, the house grew crowded once more with people from every part of the city who had heard that at Dr. Natal's there might be shelter from the war and cold. Young and old, men and women, babies crying for want of milk, they huddled together and held each other close trying to share the heat of their flesh. As they did, they told stories, whispered confidences, wept and mourned, and sometimes even laughed in the dark quiet rooms.

Finally, the day came when there were but two books left, the illustrated Bible that Bocello loved and a thin book, one so old that it sat in a place of honor upon a stone base. This book was called 'Tongue of Angels' for it was in a language no one spoke or had spoken for a thousand years. The ancient brittle pages were bound in a black hide as soft as rabbit fur. The paper, if it was paper and not some kind of skin, was so fine that when you held it you would see your fingers beneath the page. Each page was filled with a script so ornate and strange that no one knew whether to decipher it top to bottom, right to left, or contrary.

Bocello wept at the thought, certain that he could not burn either one, for they were all that was left of the great treasure of Dr. Natal; all that was left of the knowledge of the world long passed. He turned to ask the people occupying every corner of the house what he should do, but they did not know, could not agree, and would not answer. One child said, "Look to your heart," and Bocello knew that it was true.

He confessed to those in the library that if he burned these books, there would be no more, and he encouraged them to stay or to go as their conscience dictated. He did not think he could do what was required and was ready to give himself to the cold that he might join those many who had already perished.

Some did leave, and others retreated to the shadows to hold their thoughts to themselves as to whether living was still possible.

Then Bocello lay down, ready to shiver and shake his last, with the Bible like a pillow beneath his head. Once more Bocello dreamed, and Dr. Natal appeared, and said in a voice filled with great tenderness, "Books are good, rare and precious, but not nearly as precious as the life of one child. Bocello, burn the books to the very last jot of knowing."

Bocello got up. Weeping hard enough to put out the fire with his tears, he placed the Bible on the dying embers. He got down on his knees and blew gently, a soft breath that tickled a flame, and just as gently the flame reached up, and opened the very book itself. It seemed to Bocello that as each illustrated page burned it came to life so that he might see Daniel in the lion's den or the miracle of the loaves and fishes, alive and shimmering above the flames. All that he knew was there, vivid and warming.

The Bible burned for nearly a day and when it was done, Bocello went to the pedestal and removed the 'Tongue of Angels' from its honored resting place. It was surprisingly light, as if no more than a feather or a leaf rising on a breeze.

Once again, he bent to the embers to coax a flame. That's when a miracle happened. That's what Bocello would call it. That's what anyone in those walls who shivered and shook in the grip of loss would say if they were asked, "What did you see?"

What they saw was a thin book that burned bright and warmed the room for seven weeks, six days, and five hours, and when it gave up the last flicker of light, when the last wisp of smoke rose from its pages, pungent as incense; when the book was finally turned to ash, the war was over.

Gas Stop

On a dark desert highway, cool wind in my hair

Warm smell of colitas, rising up through the air

Up ahead in the distance, I saw a shimmering light

My head grew heavy and my sight grew dim

I had to stop for the night...

THE EAGLES were on the radio but though Howard and Helen were driving on a desert highway, it was not dark. There was no cool wind and the only thing in the air that late afternoon was the smell of their sun block.

The gas gauge was winking empty when Howard saw the station, or what he thought was a station, shimmering in the distance.

"We need gas."

She yawned, "We've needed gas for the last 50 miles. That doesn't look that interesting..."

"It has a pump," Howard slowed down and pulled into the driveway.

The station did have a pump. In fact, it had two old style pumps that had never seen card readers. Off to the side of the weathered adobe building, a barrel perched on a stand, complete with a hose hanging next to a sign that said, 'Diesel.'

"Primitive," Helen said. "I wonder if it's as retro inside as..." She gestured, sweeping her hand across the vista of the thick adobe walled structure with a bright red door and four tiny barred windows. Off to one side and behind the gas station was what looked like a row of ancient tourist motel rooms, though no doors were visible. On the other side stood a large metal shed, large enough to be a garage, but with a wall that slanted precariously away as if it had tried to detach itself from the rest of the building.

Howard said nothing. He got out of the car and went to the pump. There was a padlock on the nozzle. "Fuck me, what's this?"

As they entered the station, a round-bellied man with a small dark beard hanging desperately to his chin rose from a chair behind the counter. As he came around to meet them, they saw he wore a faded Grateful Dead t-shirt over tight jeans and cowboy boots that seemed to curve up to a point at the toe.

"May I be of assistance?"

"I need gas..." Howard said.

"And the pump is locked. Yes, yes, I know. It is an unfortunate necessity these days." As the station attendant spoke, he seemed to flicker as if he were a projection of some sort illuminated by a faulty bulb. "I'll get the key."

Howard was trying to place the man's accent. Something vaguely middle-eastern, not quite Arab enough to be specific, but clearly English was a second language.

Helen had been looking around the room. Ancient canned goods sat on dusty shelves and faded postcards on a spinner rack. There was a Coke machine with a carton of empty glass bottles on the floor next to it. Black and white photographs on the wall of couples, arm in arm, smiling for the camera, along with not one but three calendars. Each one showed a different month and a year that was not this year. It seemed to her to be the kind of space you'd see in a movie, the typical forgotten store on a forgotten road.

"Quaint," she said.

"Oh, I can see you don't mean that at all," said the man. "It's not your style. You're a modern couple." He laughed. "It's not my style either, but I'm stuck with it."

Howard said, "She didn't mean of offend."

The man motioned them to come closer. And as they did, he flickered again, unmistakably, becoming more solid and corporal after each brief instance of not being there. "I haven't introduced myself. I am Akbar. Yes, I know, a funny foreign name for a funny foreign man."

When he reached out, putting his hands on their arms just above the wrist, it was then all motion stopped. Neither Helen nor Howard could do more than a glance at each other or at Akbar.

"You can say your arrival here was an accident, but I know better." He smiled. "I will tell you a secret, not that it will make any difference. I am what you call a genie. In my culture, the proper term is al-jinn or djinn. This roadway station," he winked, "is my bottle, or rather, what my bottle became after it broke. Not much to your eyes, but as I will explain in a minute, there is much more here inside the bottle than you see."

Howard tried to pull away. The genie's grip on his arm only grew stronger.

"As long as I hold you, you cannot move, so you needn't speak. Just think what you will, and I'll know your thoughts."

Helen tried to not think of anything at all. But it was of no use. Thoughts came.

"I can sense your unhappiness, and I have a salve for that itch." Akbar nodded his head towards a large sign behind the counter. "Ask about our SSE services" it read, in large, hand-painted red font. Below, a smaller blue script read "Special rates for couples. Discounts for repeat users."

Helen thought it first, "What's SSE?"

Akbar laughed, "Ahh, my dear, SSE stands for Spiritual Sexual Encounters. If Howard here or any other lover does not thrill you, I can offer you the ultimate in pleasures. The eternal and ethereal made flesh for a kind of love making that leaves you satisfied to the core. I can summon a succubus, incubi, angels," he smiled broadly, "or if you prefer – djinn. Let me assure you madam that my member will be whatever length or girth you could wish for."

Helen blushed.

"Now Howard, I sensed that the angel interested you most. I have to say, I am a bit surprised. I thought you would know all angels are male in form. If an angel slept with Helen, he could also tell her whether she got pregnant after they conjoined. For you, friend, it's strictly Old Testament, Old School, with much wrestling and all that Sons of Men stuff."

Akbar leaned in to stare into Howard's eyes as if they were the windows to his soul. "You don't seem the type, though. For you I'd recommend the traditional succubus. I've got a very nice, red headed girl who can make you so hard you'll forget every promise you ever made to Helen. She'll be here as soon as you wish. She'll light a candle and show you the way to a room in back with mirrors on the ceiling and pink champagne on ice."

Howard was confused, but still lucid enough to think, "What if?" That was a wish enough for Akbar to say, "And so it is! Jezebel, come forth."

She appeared and was indeed everything that Akbar had promised. Red hair, green eyes, and shapely in all the right ways which was easy to see beneath a flowing black silk robe. She placed her hand on Howard's free arm, and as she did Akbar released his grip.

"I've reserved the fourth chamber for you two." Akbar laughed. "You're thinking, Howard, that this could be Heaven, or this could be Hell. It will probably be halfway between, or perhaps a bit of both, with what *this* Jezebel is capable of."

With that the two of them left the room, leaving Helen in Akbar's firm grip.

She had a thought and was ashamed of it but as startling as it was to her, it was even more surprising to Akbar.

"A ghost? Really – you want to sleep with a ghost?" He let go of her arm. "Do you know what you are asking?"

"Yes," she said, stepping back into enough shadow she hoped would keep Akbar from seeing the flush she felt.

"Any ghost or a particular one?"

"A particular one. My first true love." She was surprised to hear her own voice again. "Gary. Gary Madison. He was killed in Afghanistan."

"That makes it all the more complicated." Akbar ran his hand across his bald head, setting off a shower of sparks. "It is not enough that I'll have to fetch him, but I'll have to determine where to find him. There are ghosts of place and ghosts of time, and I don't suppose you know which he is."

"His place is in my heart and his time is always."

"Oh please, that kind of talk is beneath you." Akbar sat on the chair that had just moved across the room to position itself beneath him. "I'm not saying I can't do this, but my girl, this will be expensive."

"I have money."

"Money means little or nothing in this realm. In the end..." He waved his hand through the space and as he did the walls seemed to shiver, as if shaken by a highly localized earthquake. "...we are all prisoners here of our own device. What you want may not allow you to ever want anything else again."

"Do it," she said. "If you're such a fucking great djinn, give me my wish. I'll pay the price. Let me make love to Gary."

"As you wish," Akbar said. "Go through that door and to room number seven. Go inside, take off your clothes and wash in the basin that is there. Then light the sandalwood incense that sits beside the basin and wait."

Helen asked, "Where is he?"

"He'll be along. It might take a while but once you are in the room, time won't matter."

She turned towards the door, which opened as she approached it. Walking the corridor, she thought she heard voices at every door. Room seven had a black door made of what appeared to be charred wood. It opened as she reached for the handle. She entered, and time collapsed.

The room was like a room in a dream, not quite in focus, except for a basin resting on a small table alongside the large bed with black sheets, which were turned down and waiting to receive their bodies. There did not seem to be windows or a source of light, but the room was a mix of soft illumination and moving shadows.

After Helen completed the ritual washing and lighting of the sandalwood, she grew impatient. But long had it been? Although naked, she stood in the doorway listening to a distant bell. It sounded four times.

"Helen." a strained voice spoke behind her. "Close the door."

When she turned, Gary was in the room and yet, he was not. Like Akbar, he seemed to be flickering, both there and not there at the same time. She reached out to take his hand,

and hers seemed to sink through Gary's flesh rather than stop at the skin. He flickered again, and when she looked a second time, her hand was holding his corporeal form. He appeared to be fully there.

Helen kissed him. He returned the kiss in a distracted sort of way, as if he was trying to remember how to kiss. Or why...

"Is something wrong, love?"

"The body. It feels so heavy, so...limiting."

"Please, Gary, just be here with me. I'll make you happy to be in your body again."

He stretched, beginning with the arches of his feet and then up the legs, hips, spine, shoulders, and finally head, all rising as muscles flexed as if pulling everything into alignment.

She looked at his naked body. He was exactly how she remembered him except for the eyes that would not look at her, but instead gazed past her, to some middle space beyond. She pulled him towards her, close enough that his penis pressed against her labia. She reached out with one hand to stroke it to erection. Unlike the first time they made love, those many years ago on his parent's couch, he was slow to respond.

"Do you love me, Gary, like I love you?"

"Yes, Helen, I've always loved you. And now it is pure."

"I don't want pure love at this moment, I want the carnal. I want your arms around me, your lips everywhere they can reach, your flesh in mine," and with a half turn she pulled him to the bed.

It seemed to Helen that Gary was at last coming fully into his body. He began to hold her close, placing his hands on her buttocks, squeezing them, then lightly slapping her ass. His mouth did go everywhere it could reach. His erect member took her attention, pressing here and there, and when he entered her, it was not the way he had in their youth but with an authority that surprised her. Her excitement built and when she climaxed it was not once, but repeatedly, one shuddering spasm after another with her calling his name and God's until she thought she would be hoarse.

"Stop, stop, please, in God's name, let me rest."

He withdrew and as he did, she saw that he was still fully erect.

"Did you come?"

"No. I have no reason to spill seed," he said, looking at her. "This was for your pleasure, for the satisfaction of the body's hunger."

"And yours." She asked in a voice small enough to be a whisper, "Isn't it for your pleasure as well?"

"My pleasure," Gary laughed, "is not the pleasure of the body but the co-joining of the spirit. When you leave the mortal plane, abandon the temple of flesh, I will be able to fuse with you, essence to essence, and in that our pleasure will be complete."

"Oh Gary, that is what I want, what I wish for...to always be together."

The very moment after she spoke these words, Akbar was standing next to the bed. "By the Prophet, you are a handsome couple!" He looked at Gary and ran a finger across the well-defined chest. "I can see why you wanted him back."

"What are you doing here?"

"You made your last wish, and I am here to set the terms for its completion." He sat down on the edge of the bed. Helen pulled the black sheet up to cover herself, but Akbar reached out and pulled it away. "It is too late for that modesty. Now listen closely to me for this is a delicate matter. Do you believe that taking your own life is a sin and if you did so, your God would condemn you to eternal damnation?"

"No. Why are you asking that?"

"You wished to always be with Gary. He, however, is not condemned to eternal damnation. For the two of you to be together, you must pass through the veil in a manner that will put you in the same spiritual realm as him. If you believe, he must also be damned. But if you do not believe, taking your life is no matter."

Helen blinked and looked at Gary, whose head was resting on his arm as if he were watching sports or a light-hearted comedy. "And my taking my life is...."

"The easiest way to get you to the next realm. But as I said, your belief in the afterlife or lack thereof makes a difference as to how it must be done in order to achieve what the desired result will be"

"I was taught that suicide is a sin."

"Well there we have it. However, by the grace of all that is Holy there is a way around that," Akbar said. "Gary, how did you die?"

"A wall collapsed on me – crushed, killed, buried me in one motion."

"Helen. It is Helen, right? Full given name? You made the wish and I am going to fulfill it as stated, but since you believe or believed that suicide is a sin, and I do like the opinionated woman that you are, I'm going to bend the rules of my profession slightly to make this work."

"No suicide?" Helen looked at Akbar who was stroking his beard and staring at the ceiling.

"No." he said. "And I think that Gary can remain. In fact, I think Gary should resume coitus with you, and that you, Helen, should be on top."

"And?"

"Oh, I don't want to spoil the surprise." He kissed his hand and then put his fingers to her lips. Helen closed her eyes and felt a warm kiss with just the slightest suggestion of tongue. When she opened them, Akbar was gone.

Gary took her foot and massaging it as he did, he began to suck on her toes but soon moved to her ankle, her calf, then turning her over he kissed the back of her knee which made her giggle. He continued alternately kissing and licking her thigh, her buttocks and the region between her legs.

Helen gripped the still erect phallus and guided him onto his back. She straddled him and as she was guiding his penis in, she did not see the large chandelier with heavy glass spikes worthy of Chihuly that materialized above the bed.

As she climaxed, the ceiling fell.

It seemed to Helen that one moment she was in her body, flush with pleasure and suddenly she was outside her body, looking at a single human form in the bed, bleeding, with glass spikes like porcupine quills protruding from her back and shoulders.

Before she could react, she was aware of a luminous form reaching for her. Though it did not have a human face, she knew this was the essence of Gary. Helen turned and as she did, their spectral hands met and merged. Arms followed and then the whole of their shimmering forms. One into the other with residual atoms colliding, exchanging energy, making little sparks of light as if they were living Fourth of July sparklers.

The sensation was divine.

Akbar sat in his chair and smiled at the thought that she got her wish. He chuckled. No tricks there. His Grateful Dead t-shirt disappeared and was replaced by a collarless starched white shirt. "And now for Howard," he said, to no one.

In the fourth chamber, Howard sat on the edge of the bed furiously dialing numbers in hopes the phone he found there would work. Jezebel had left the bed and was back in her black silk robe swaying to some music he did not hear in front of a full-length mirror.

"Come Howard, dance with me." She called out.

"I'm trying to get us something to drink. Wine, whiskey, water, anything..."

Akbar appeared with a small tray in hand. "We haven't had a decent wine here since nineteen sixty-nine." He placed the tray on the table, "Here, this is pretty good mescal. I make it myself from plants behind the shed."

He continued, "And how are you Howard? Is she all that I promised?"

Howard poured himself a glass and swallowed it in one sip.

"Really, Howard, take your time. Savor it." Akbar said, "You're not in a rush. There's plenty of time." He laughed. "In fact, there's nothing *but* time in this space."

"I have to go," Howard said. "We have to go. Where's Helen?"

"Ahh, yes. That is what I've come to talk to you about. Helen... hmmm... let's just say that she has left the building. Such a sweet girl, she wanted me to give you her good-byes. You won't be seeing her again."

"What do you mean, she's left the building?" Howard stood and made a fist as if he could threaten Akbar. "Left when? How? With who?"

Akbar looked at the fist. He put out his hand to cover Howard's and straightened the coiled fingers out again. "Really, Howard, you need to let go of that anger impulse. It will not serve you well here. If you really want to indulge, I can move you over to room nine where the angry ones gather. It's such a fucking waste of time."

Akbar motioned to Jezebel who came over and leaned forward slightly to let him put his arm around her shoulders. Akbar seeing her stooped position grew a few inches taller so she could stand upright.

"Now this one, this Jezebel, besides knowing and being willing to perform the entire vast encyclopedia of sexual pleasures, perversions and possibilities, also has a lot of pretty, pretty boys that she calls friends who like dancing in the courtyard. Some dance to remember and some dance to forget. You could be one of them."

"We were talking about Helen, Akbar. Forget Jezebel for a moment and tell me about Helen."

"Well she made the third wish, and I fulfilled it." Akbar gave Jezebel a little kiss on the cheek and patted her behind. As she vanished, he spread his hands in a gesture that implied there is nothing more.

"What do you mean, she made THE third wish?"

Akbar poured another glass of mescal and handed it to him. "You might want this. You know how it goes, how the stories are told. Three wishes granted. True enough. So when the two of you entered my humble abode, you got three wishes."

"So what? I've only made one so far."

"True. You made the first wish. Then Helen made one and then, just a few minutes or a few hours ago, it doesn't really matter when, she made the third wish." Akbar leaned in to look at Howard. "It was NOT three wishes apiece. You came in as a couple and according to the rules, it was three wishes between the two of you."

Howard looked at the glass and brought it to his lips, hesitated, "What the fuck are you saying?"

"Plain and simple – you are out of wishes."

"Then I'll just leave."

"Well, that's where it gets sticky. You know that old song, Hotel California?"

"What of it?" Howard reached out to pour himself a third mescal.

"How does that last stanza go?" Akbar hummed a little bit then in a surprisingly strong voice sang:

"'Relax,' said the night man, 'we are programmed to receive.'

'You can check out any time you like, but you can never leave!'"

"And that's pretty much where we're at now. Helen did not include you in her departure wish and you don't have a wish to work with. On the bright side, you have Jezebel's ministrations for as long as you're here."

"How is that possible?"

"Really Howard, you're asking how any of this is possible *now?* You're inside my bottle. It is the conjunction of two irreconcilable and implausibly different worlds that are contained much like a nuclear reaction within a vessel. In here all things are possible, though the truth is I can't get out without being called from outside and if I can't get out, you can't either."

"I'll try..."

"Be my guest." Akbar laughed. "Oh, wait, you are my guest and perhaps we should talk about how a good guest is not ungrateful for their welcome. Do you like the mescal? As I said I make it myself and I could use some help."

Meeting Myself

"THE ESSENTIAL PROBLEM with time travel is that you can't go back and kill Hitler. It's like that famous story, 'The Sound of Thunder' by Ray Bradbury where the dinosaur hunter steps on a butterfly and changes the outcome of the election. Every change you make in the past alters your present and in practical terms argues against time travel."

Giselle nodded absently. "I understand that, but my interest in time travel is not to alter the past but to confirm it. You wouldn't necessarily have to physically be there to be able to observe and even to record what happened."

"That's the focus of your research work?" Her doctoral committee chair frowned. "You're going to posit this as a theory with supporting calculations?"

"No, I'm going to actually do it with documentation."

"No one has done it. I won't say it can't be done but..." The committee chair trailed off, then added, "I will say that's awfully ambitious, but then you are one of the most ambitious students we have ever had in the neuroscience program." He stood to leave her office. "If you succeed it will be worth a Nobel but remember your research funding will end in three years and I won't be able to get you more without some evidence of progress."

Her approach was simple enough. To project consciousness back through time to observe the past and to record via neural chips what was seen and heard by that consciousness. What was observed would be induced through a combination of carefully formulated drugs and electrical stimulation. The resulting activity would then be recorded and digitally organized to present on screen what was being experienced in the visual and auditory spheres.

The tricky part was, she realized how to have it be an actual progression and not just an imagined one. It had taken her months to work out the elements and assemble a projection system.

In the earliest stage, she had graduate students go into the near past, to a time before they were born but within the lifespan of those still living. She had university colleagues in their 60's and 70's interviewed about their childhood homes, schools, towns. Then she meticulously built what she called the "collaborating evidence" that would lend support to those memories, but be unknown to a twenty-something who had lived with an often indistinguishable jumble of virtual realities.

She would set the test subjects into the chair wearing goggles and headphones. The students often assumed they were testing some new game and would be eager to find the items she asked them to look for. Once they were sent to the selected chronological and spatial coordinates, she would record what they saw and heard for later comparison to the documented database.

The experiments worked better than she expected, but while the results showed very high correlations between the projection techniques and the arrival targets, she became unsatisfied with simply auditing what has happened in a known destination.

Giselle was sure that with modification of the apparatus she could boost the signal and move further into the past. It took another year before they were able to reach back to Germany in 1936 to directly observe the Berlin Olympics. Ambitiously, they then tried to reach China in 1644 and the ascension of the Qing Dynasty capturing Beijing. What was observed in that session was entirely new material, since the historical record was mostly names and artifacts. It now could include the look and sound of the Banner Armies marching through Shanghai Pass. What she captured was the stuff of an epic movie or what could be made into an epic movie if you downplayed the actual bloodletting and added a love interest.

Yet every step forward did not seem to be enough. Giselle resolved to find a way to physically manifest in another time. She again reconfigured the mechanism to allow a kind of holographic image to materialize. On the plus side, the graduate students were thrilled to be able to "walk" the streets of the target destinations. On the negative side even when the computers clothed them in what was assumed to be period attire, they did not always have the appropriate clothing to pass as a native of the time and place. This especially caused problems involving race and gender roles during what they all agreed were excursions to the "barbaric" past.

Try as she might, while she was able to manifest the appearance of physical simulation in another era, they had not figured out a way to allow for speech or to physically pick up an object or eat food. As she put it, "We are no better than moving mannequins."

That was fine with the university's research oversight committee. As pleased as they were at her developing the methodology, as well as the machinery for what promised to be wealth producing patents and the potential of licensing time travel, they repeatedly warned her about altering the past. Several committee members believed that eating, drinking, picking up a tool or weapon, or even, and most critically, engaging in conversation with observed subjects, would alter the timeline and that could not be allowed.

Then it hit her. If she projected a subject into the future any effect of alteration of time travel would already be manifest. It meant going back to her previous technique, but in the first experiment she was able to project a graduate student's consciousness and observational power a week into the future and record the daily news. When the week elapsed, their success was confirmed. She was elated and immediately wanted to move a month or more into the future.

On in the third try when they projected six months into the future, she was unaware that the subject who made the "ascension" as they called it, had also observed the stock market. Upon his return, he made several small and strategic investments. These proved so lucrative that Charles, the test subject, asked Giselle for another opportunity to ascend.

When pressed as to why, the reason came out. Although Giselle should surely have seen it as an ethical red flag, she considered it confirmation of the success of the technique. Further tests put consciousness a year, two and then five years into the future.

Having projected consciousness, Giselle wanted to try once again for a hologram likeness of the body that was capable of movement. She had been working on a new set of calculations that she thought would allow the projected self to speak. To move and interact with the world that had yet to be. Oh, how she wanted to accomplish that. It was at that moment she did what every scientist in every horror movie does to ill effect. She decided to abandon the protocols and become the subject herself.

Moreover, she decided to push the calculated limits of ascension capacity, setting it twenty years into the future. This would be the crowning achievement of her work, proof that a version of bodily time travel had been achieved. It would allow the scientific community to directly learn from the future and therefore accelerate its arrival. If she was truly successful, she believed that she would not be the only time traveler arriving and departing from the new world, she would simply be the first of many.

Having thought at some length about the problem of where to go, she selected a site that would probably still be there in twenty years, largely unchanged. Grant Park in Chicago.

Giselle could feel the anticipation rising as her lab assistant clipped on the neural sensors. This would be what she had worked for all these years. The repudiation of the naysayers and her achievement would rank her with Einstein and Hawking.

At first it was like a dream, the room fading from view and after a few anxious seconds Chicago shimmering into focus. She looked down to see her hands. Moved them. Yes, she looked to be solid and even felt it. Excitement built as she heard the sounds of the city. She stared at a skyline that was both familiar and changed, with giant screens projecting ads and public art.

Someone called her name. Who was it? The moment was historical – why wouldn't someone be there to greet her? A news reporter or another time traveler? She turned to see a woman. Not any woman, but herself, now twenty years older. She had not expected that, but it made of sense. She would know the time and place of her arrival. Why not come to congratulate yourself on such an achievement?

"I've waited a long time for this, Giselle."

"And here we are..."

"No, here *you* are," the older Giselle said, "and I'm sorry to say, here you will stay."

"What do you mean?"

"You're a ghost." She reached out to touch the projected Giselle and her hand passed through the arm with a little ripple as if it was nothing more than standing water.

"But..."

"No, don't say that this worked. It would only be half true. Yes, you have just crossed the temporal barrier and we are speaking. Congratulations on solving that problem. I don't know if you can pick up an object or eat a piece of fruit as much as you might want, or rather wanted to be able to do so. You'll have to test that after we finish this conversation, but it won't make a difference. The truth is, this experiment is failing."

"What do you mean?" The younger Giselle felt a wave of panic. She was here and she was speaking. She could observe, she could move. If it was failing, she didn't know how but she would need to correct it. When to correct it? Now? When she returned? Was there some way to signal the lab assistant as she sat in the subject chair? To do what?

"You were able to come here but you never came back."

"Never came back?" Her sense of panic grew. "What do you mean? I can see your body – MY body..."

"When the system cycled through the allotted 30 minutes for your being here, you did not return. To be more precise, which I know you'll appreciate, at the end of the 30 minutes the system stopped recording but while my body – OUR body – was sitting in the chair, there was no evidence that the projected consciousness had returned. I lost cognitive function and was, in effect, in a coma for nearly a year."

"You recovered, though." The projected Giselle looked at the older one. There was something about her that was familiar, and yet – it was as if she were missing something.

"Yes, I recovered cognition and basic bodily functions. Or so they told me." The elder Giselle reached into a pocket and pulled out a cigarette case. Opening it, she lit up a cigarette, or rather a joint. "Funny, this was made fully legal a decade ago and I've been on a prescribed dose since the week I regained consciousness." She took a long drag and exhaled. "I smoke to offset panic. Maybe the same panic I suspect you are feeling now. That fear stayed in the body even when the knowing was missing, but what did I know? It was missing"

"But here's the thing, honey, when I finally recovered consciousness, everything that I knew about my work was gone. Well, that's not quite right either. Everything that was not documented, all the pieces of calculation and process that you kept to yourself were with you, here, twenty years in the future."

"You know – well actually, you don't know, because you're in this time and I was in a coma in that one – the project was shut down by the research oversight committee after I was taken to the hospital. I suppose someone could have argued for an attempt to find you, to get you back, but try as I might, once I came to, I couldn't make any sense of what was left."

"I had to give it all up – the project, the theories, the thought of a Ph.D. I had to take what was left of me and recreate the semblance of a life. Do you remember Charles? The test subject who parleyed his glimpse of the future into a small fortune? He was, and is, appreciative of what you, I, did and brought me on as a partner.

"While a lot of your gifts... yes, I think that's the word. While a lot of your gifts left with you, I must say that my computational and mathematical analytic capacity remained ingrained. It's served me and Charles quite well."

"What will happen to me?" Giselle was suddenly aware of the enormity of her troubles.

"I have no idea; how long can you remain here or what will you do?" The older version of herself laughed. "I suppose I could invite you home with me. Could you ride in the tube? Can you cross the threshold of my condo or are you fixed in these coordinates? That will have to be discovered. We could have a cup of tea, or can we? I could ask you about all those secrets you kept out of the logs and notes, but really, your failure to come back then pretty much ended all enthusiasm for time travel. Mine or anybody else's.

"You should be famous as one of the most spectacular failures in the history of the University, in all of science, for that matter, you should be an object lesson in hubris except for the cover-up. Your ambition could not be allowed even a footnote in the history books. The university couldn't afford to answer the questions that would be asked, and I felt such shame that I was you, even in a diminished form, that I was not about to ask anything."

Giselle's eyes were wide, her voice barely louder than a whisper. "You have to help me..."

"Do I?" The older woman took another drag of the sweet-smelling marijuana. "Your ambition did me no favors. Well, maybe Charles is the exception that proves the rule. But really, you rushed to this time and space and here you are for who knows how long. Can't go back. Didn't go back. I made my peace with your failure and made my way in this harsh world without access to who I was from the moment you sat in that chair. No, I don't think I owe you anything. I certainly don't want anything from you *now*."

Turning, the older Giselle then walked away, leaving her ghostly self behind. All that was left for the younger Giselle was to make her way for however long she had in this mysterious new world. But there had to be a solution. She could move, she could interact, she could communicate. She would find someone – anyone – who might have continued her research, and then convince them to send her back. She would find a way to change the past.

That is, if she had enough time.

The Ghost in the Machine

LATE ONE NIGHT, a ghost came through the wall, passing through the computer that was sitting on the desk. It was nothing more than an ephemeral shimmer of light, as if the very molecules of air brushed against each other, sparking as they did.

At first, I thought the passage of the specter made no difference. It was as insubstantial as the flicker of a firefly's wink, a thin envelope of gleaming phosphorescent spirit more suggestion than movement, a mere hint of presence rather than an actual form, and its passage didn't seem to affect anything – at least not immediately.

When I turned the computer on to check it, it kicked in as it always did. It was only later that the behavior of the computer suggested the wandering, dislocated spirit had somehow rearranged internal connections, and in so doing altered the orderly arrangement of 1 and 0 which is the province of machine memory. The passage of spiritual energy between this visible plane and the intangible one had apparently disturbed several machine circuits and caused a kind of processing hiccup, which manifested with the computer performing seemingly random actions.

Bits of text would show up, some of which I had written, and some of which I could not identify. One of the first of these was an old piece from one of my journals, a scene long-forgotten from my college days in southern Minnesota. This particular entry was my report on the final dregs of a wedding which took place on a hot June day.

After the vows in the white clapboard chapel, after the toasts and fried chicken dinner in the Town Hall basement, and sometime before the tossing of the bouquet to the squealing gaggle of girlfriends, the Best Man joined Big Jack, Big Jack's dog, and me for a little respite in the form of a drive through the rolling wooded hills in search of another kind of fun. A fast drive down a two-lane blacktop highway on a summer's night, the farm fields appearing out of the darkness, their ordered green rows of corn caught in the headlights and then racing past the open windows with a flicker of leaves vibrating in the heat as they leapt back into the dark. The car was filled with the smell of sweet growth, the smell of the tall grasses and wild flowers in the roadside ditches.

This was the night Big Jack showed us how to smoke hashish without a pipe. That old pirate just reached into his pocket and pulled out a lump of black something at least the size of a golf ball. With a single magnanimous gesture, Big Jack had presented us with another kind of fun in the form of a tarry souvenir from his last trip to Morocco or Lebanon. Push in the cigarette lighter, pinch off a sliver of the black ball, drop it onto the glowing coil. Snort the small white cloud that appeared straight off the lighter. Nothing to it, just inhale a little smoke and a hot coal of hash right up the sinus cavities. Burned all the way up.

They say drugs kill. Got that right. Common sense and excess nose hair died in an instant. Shit, the pain was intense, but the effect was more than curious. It gave new meaning to the word "rush".

Whammm! Suddenly the windshield was no longer a curved surface moving through a three-dimensional landscape but a huge flat screen on which a cartoon version of the world was projected. Blink and look again. The car was still racing through the night, the speedometer winking at us from the high end of seventy-five, but we did not seem to be moving. I knew this was the case, because the sound of the wind roaring through the windows had ceased. The trees with the crickets singing on their branches no longer came and went but were replaced by one silhouette of a tree after another, each as flat as a paper cut-out, separate and equal in their many suggestions of what a tree ought to look like, moving in slow stately procession. The yellow lines wiggled, wiggled, and at last floated up off the road, casting shadows that in turn fluttered like frightened bats in the headlights. And then Mickey Mouse came racing across the screen and grabbed the lines, snapped them like a whip and laid them back down on the black asphalt receding to a visible point in the distance like every illustration of perspective I had ever seen in art school.

A hundred shooting stars, red, green, neon blue, like tracers from a fire fight, zigzagged across the sky as Big Jack says, "Jesus, this is pretty good shit."

I look at this text floating on the computer screen. There is nothing more to it though there should have been.

I remember how the rest of that story goes. Twenty years later I recall that precise moment, and the aftermath of that precise moment, which now exists outside the bounds of physical chronology. A moment etched deep in the brain, unexamined, nearly forgotten but still very much present, shimmering with emotion and intent. The Best Man wanted a drink. He howled at the night, raised his hands from the steering wheel and declared that he wanted to go to his favorite bar in Eyota, the one with the piranha in the fish tank. He wanted to feed french fries to the always hungry fish. He wanted to be far away from the chapel when the groom left because when men marry, they are lost to the company of men no matter what they say.

It was a long drive, or at least seemed that way. In fact, it was only a few miles from our point of departure, but in a universe of expanding space and collapsing time measured by three pinches of hash, the road was endless. And the light years of that journey were soon joined by an unspoken panic that oncoming traffic was repeatedly weaving into our lane or backing up to come at us a second time.

We hit the curb as we approximated parking the car. A crash echoed off the quiet bricks of a town that believed in early to bed, early to rise. When we walked in the dark paneled bar, the farmers in summer work shirts and sweat stained bib overalls smelling of manure and sour milk turned their heads as a single unit to look us over. "Fucking...long haired college kids," they muttered to themselves and turned back to stare at the big screen baseball game.

The computer does not wait for me to finish reading that story but scrolls the screen to display pieces of another, equally fragmented text; one I wrote about my twenty-five-year-old girlfriend, half my age, in the middle of a bitter January night. A text that prefigured all the reasons she would offer when she dumped me. A text that begins:

She has made few, if any, declarations of emotional commitment to us except to say "more" when I ask what I can do to increase her pleasure. I am a convenience, a distraction, some kind of refuge from the inconsiderate and too anxious men her own age.

Do I want to read what comes next? To be reminded of my foolishness? No, better to turn away from the screen and go back to that other year, that other man I once was, who was more open hearted than this self on the page in front of me.

Man, them piranhas were something to behold with a head full of hash. They seemed not to swim so much as float in a universe that was not water, but something more substantial, thick like green Jell-O, giving off phosphorescent trails as they struggled to swim the length of the tank. They would hesitate before the glass, and then turn slowly back to circumnavigate that thickness once more. The Best Man stared at the fish. Their mouths opened and shut like little metronomes, the sharp little teeth calling out from a hunger that was instinctual, calling out for the taste of blood. The Best Man's mouth was opening and closing in the same rhythm, but his hunger was pharmacological, not instinctual.

Meanwhile, Jack's dog was pacing back and forth, wanting to leave the smoky confines of the place. The dog had a wooden leg that gave its movement an odd time signature – thump, thump, thump, thunk. Thump, thump, thump, thunk. I was listening to the dog walk and thought that there was a kind of music there. A defiance of Fate, or a statement of will that would not give up, sounding in the animal's restless movement between Big Jack and the door. He longed for the freedom of the dark and wild, and if we had any sense we would have as well.

My girlfriend liked to argue with me against the notion of freedom and for a determinism that is the result of X and Y, of paired chromosomes and genetics, of the eight hundred million or more inputs reinforcing X and Y from birth. In her view, it was both nature and nurture. We cannot be other than we are and must do what we will do.

By that logic, I could not help but kiss her, and once I kissed her all that followed must have been. Though the romance would arc from thrill to disaster, she did not see it as unexpected. If anything, in her deterministic world she could trace the future from that first kiss. By that logic, she would commit or not commit to our relationship no matter what I did.

By that logic, the dog must always want to go outside. By that logic, when I was presented with Big Jack's smoky invitation to see reality from a different perspective, the rush was already hard-wired in my nerves, and the expansion of consciousness that came from a deconstruction of that summery world was already implied and merely waiting for permission to manifest itself.

I hit the erase button and sent both texts to oblivion. There was no point in dwelling on what I had said about her then or now. That was a lesson learned. The other? The story of men, dogs, and fish was entertaining at the time, but not now. I needed to be in this present, figuring out the effect of this ghost in this machine. Could it be exorcised? Consigning these tales to the half-life of decaying electrons that languish in the primordial pool of the computer's memory was called for. If only they would stay gone.

Photographs then appeared on screen. I recognized every one of them. I had taken each one at some time or another. At first they seemed random, but then I began to recognize a pattern in the presentation of the images. A pattern that was taking me back, further and further from the present into the past and allowing the dead to appear.

There was a picture of a woman I had known for many years. She's long dead now, but in the photo she's smiling, she's at a picnic, she's on a blanket holding a glass of wine and looking at the camera, still forty-two years old. Five years after the photo was taken, her life would be claimed.

Here is the picture of a guy I had worked with, who had drowned in an accident. He's standing with a canoe paddle on the shore of the St. Croix River. In the picture, we are about start kayaking from Stillwater to Hudson. It would be the last time we were together.

The images appeared one after another after another, each in succession, further and further back in time until I arrived at the first photo of the first person I ever knew who had died. A picture of my grandfather and grandmother, sitting. Well, she's sitting on the running board of a '34 Ford and he's leaning on the fender. I look at the photograph, I examine it, and at last enlarge it, making it bigger and bigger until the pixels become more prominent than the image, to discern in what ways he is me.

I recognize that he and I both have the same moustache. His hair is longer, his eyes seem keener, but we have the same slouch. I wonder, if the ghost in the machine is *his* ghost, and in what way I am the continuation of him, his ghost internalized in my blood and bone.

The ghost came through the wall and through the computer that was sitting on the desk in front of the wall. Bits of text would show up, some of which I had written and some of which I could not identify where they had been downloaded from, how they had come to be in the machine. But I soon discovered that this presentation of unrequested texts, arbitrarily presented and oddly intertwined like reoccurring dreams, was not the only result of the spirit's passage. It seems the ghost had also left a message in the program that appeared at random intervals when I used the printer. Always the same message:

Why am I alone?

The words might appear at the beginning or the end, or sometimes in the middle of other texts. Once at the edges of a page, a single word appearing in each one of the corners:

Why   am

I   alone?

I read and re-read the words, wanting to answer the spirit's message, to ease the pain I thought the question revealed. If I can do so, I considered, maybe it will heal the rift that has been forged within the landscape of my hard drive. I begin to think about the reality of *why* and *I*. About the mystery that is *us*, both alone and still in want and need of companionship.

As I contemplate the question my brain is active, electro-chemical stimulations firing off bits of nerve impulse, bits of pattern recognition interpreted as – what?

A whole? A thought? A memory? An answer?

On, off, yes, no. In the computer the world is reduced to one and zero. Every question, every answer formatted as a combination of 1 and 0, such as 11001100. How different is that from my own processes of thought and memory? Is my world any more than the sum of X and Y? Is my genetic base of paired chromosomes, the linked yes and no of every question that determines the self? Height, weight, male or female, blue eyes or brown, white or black skin; are these anything more than the process or the accumulation of a biological 1 and 0 in the organic processor?

> *What is thought? What is this language? What is this ritual magic I use to conjure the question, much less to conjure an answer?*

The ghost passed through the machine and asked, *why am I alone?* Perhaps that's not the right question. I look at these hands sitting on the keyboard, moving keys, moving atoms from one time and place to another, making meaning with a consciousness that is singular but also a part of *we* who call ourselves human, *we* who call ourselves alive. This consciousness attributes meaning to words and words to concepts, and concepts to emotions and actions that in the aggregate are bounded by culture.

And still I ask, when are we ever really alone? I took the paper and crossed those words out. *Wrong,* I said, *wrong.* Perhaps I read it in the wrong order. Might it be better understood as "Alone am I why...?"

Letters form – a line, a curve, an intentionally ordered difference set against a random or uniformly ignored background, a symbol that carries within itself only line, but to which a meaning is nonetheless assigned. Letters are a veritable cornucopia of associative history assumed and unquestioned.

This is -w.

This is -h.

This is -y.

Even as isolated bits, as a path from point to point they carry meaning if we give them meaning. They are recognized and assigned a value, ordered and given sensibility. Joined until they acquire a meaning that is a sum of their parts – or more than the sum of their parts.

W-H-Y is not only a string of three letters. It suggests something outside the immediate bonds of their union. It is a word. WHY. All that is humanity's genius and limitation may be found in those three letters. WHY? 000011101101.

What is the half-life of decay, the half-life of memory? Computers rearrange electrons. Do we not also rearrange words and memories in relation to our sensory input? Objectively, a word or a memory has no meaning until I *make* it mean something.

And yet that particular question, *Why am I alone,* means something.

In that long-ago time, I looked at the blank screen of the car windshield and saw the world projected, not as a continuum of weight, shape and spatial relationship, but as discrete pieces – colors with equal values, forms without depth. Now, I look at the monitor and see that the digital world is also a flat surface, transforming internal to external, a phosphorescent projection of one and zero as a discernible pattern of letters floating on an electron sea.

I look again at the past and the present. I close my eyes and consider again my being in the world, of a world or worlds, simultaneous and equally present worlds, fitting together the binary of 100111010101 into a recognizable whole. How are they different? In observation this world has shape and form, color and substance. In memory, it has shape and form, color and substance.

Enter the space of memory and enter the X and Y of yes or no, on or off, to taste the cold beer once again washing away the thick half-life of the Moroccan sun in a puff of white smoke. In the space of memory, do I actually taste that, or do I just remember the pleasure of tasting it? What really matters when I enter these memories? That world is as much a ghost as any.

I will the world into being, giving the internal command to make it manifest, over and over again. Hundreds of times a second, assembling bits and pieces, the X and the Y, the one and the zero of the known universe, and then ignore all the data that is inconvenient when the chosen and self-ordered world is manifest. I ignore the discomfort of too much information, the discomfort of unwanted emotion. *Put it aside for later.* Where there is not enough, I fill in the blanks with assumption and probability. I assign a pattern of what should be to the suggestion of what might be.

Look at this hand. It is the connection between man and machine. Look at this hand. It is not spirit, but it conjures and contains spirit.

Make the words appear.

In the brain I say, let us go back to another time, another place and make it visible again. Let us gather that long past living into the present, travel in time with a few keystrokes and explore the emotions, feel the visceral sensations again. It is not the same moment but another, richer moment, charged with who I was then and who I have become now. Stimulate the neurons and the flood of memory comes. Internalized. I can see us sitting in that bar, with the dog pacing the floor – *thump, thump, thump, thunk* – and us watching fish like they were the secret to all understanding.

In the brain I can say, I know why I wanted to sleep with her youth, to feel the smooth promise of her skin next to my experience and inhale her intoxicating scent. I could guess or project her reasons, choose to give them weight or ignore them. What matter did it make when we were limbs entangled in the pleasure of the moment?

So that it could be remembered and celebrated. So it could be longed for when she was gone.

I look at my hands. Oh, what a wonder this machine of flesh and desire is! They are the link, the intentionality between past and present. Opposable thumbs; the tool making capacity inherent. Count to ten. Form follows function. All the possibility of now is in the DNA of a single embrace, the first kiss or the first fuck, the first joining of possibility.

The fingers reach across the arrangement of keys and prompt the machine. Push the -w. Push the -h. Push the -y. Shift. Push the -?

00110100011100101010101010101. The bits do their work in the realm of machine life and letters flicker on the blank screen. It is all a continuum.

Whose hands are these? When did this scar first appear? Where did these wrinkles come from? Is it really all a continuum? Time folds in upon itself and the hands that are before me are, or are not, the hands that held the hot cigarette lighter with the pinch of hot wind and sun rising to tickle the edge of my nostril. These are, or are not, the gentle hands that entered the soft folds of her wet pleasure to make her smile and ask for more. How would I know? In my internal pattern recognition processor are these, or are these not, the same hands that held the beer, that held the sleeping beauty in the candle lit bedroom, that touched the dog's rough coat, that typed the word, why? What remains of X and O?

The texts came back, even after I tried to erase them. They came back. The memories returned as if they had never left, and in fact they remained, even though they might be denied or altered by time or emotion. All the photos came back. The dead came back. Always and again, their names reappear and for every name, a face.

The dead are always with us if we but say their names. I want to say to the ghost that we are not alone. Here this physical body, this biology of molecules and atoms stacked one upon the other, and held together by what? By habit? By genetics? By will? By ghostly spirit?

When I die the atoms are freed from one form to another. They begin to rearrange themselves, but they are still there. They are always there. There are no new atoms, no atoms go missing. Every atom from the first moment of creation to the end of time is still with us. Whether it is here in the corporal body, in the sinew or blood, in the wall, in the air, in the electrons sizzling on the screen, or in the printer spelling out "Why am I alone?"

If we look at atoms we are not alone, we are multitudes crowded in a thousand forms, but atoms all the same. The space between is filled with us. So what are we?

And when I die, that which is not atoms, that other thing – what is that?

Consciousness, curiosity, spirit, soul – call it what you will. The thing that arranges, that takes these atoms held into some semblance of who we are is not *only* who we are. There is that thing which asks *Why am I alone* and it is not the atoms. The atoms do not speak that.

What is that other thing?

If I turn to religions that say we are made in God's likeness, I then have to say it's not the corporal, it's not the body. It's the other thing. That which is here and is not here, the shimmer of energy that can pass through the wall and the computer. That which asks the question, and says *I am.* That which is in the body, and separate from the body, and aware of the body all at the same time.

That self which is even able to ask, "Why am I alone?" As if you are in denial of the fact that you *are* – in a singular moment not aware of yourself as living or dead, as here or there – reaching out to another to be reassured. That spirit which may not yet be aware of death or in denial of it, and which is seeking the answer to the *Why* that none of us can ever be sure of but is still asking, still seeking.

The seeking itself marks us as different from atoms.

Late one night, a ghost came through the wall, passing through the computer that was sitting on the desk. It was nothing more than an ephemeral shimmer of light, as if the very molecules of air brushed against each other, sparking as they did.

Dating the Vampire

SHE WAS IN NO HURRY to leave even if it was time for him to close the office. If anything, she settled more comfortably into the chair, and pulled a cigarette out of her purse. She launched into a dizzy story about how she arrived from New York and needed a little help finding her way around. She was wearing a low-cut black cocktail dress that left plenty of good leg exposed. She wore no wedding ring, and he liked the idea of getting lost in eyes like Hale-Bopp shining on a clear night. He was hooked, line and sinker.

They hit it off right away. He was Lancelot mounting a white steed. Moving from his office in City Hall to a dark wood paneled bar, they settled into an easy banter. Here, let me get you another bone-dry martini. Out came the little book of contacts, and favors got called in. So what if on the second day she quit the marketing job he found for her, complaining that it was demeaning to have to go to work in the morning? She kept the apartment he found and encouraged his passionate devotion to her pleasure at every wrong turn.

It was soon clear she was only truly happy after nightfall, preferring a darkened apartment with tightly drawn shades and '50's jazz on the stereo. When a sliver of exhausted sun creased the horizon, she'd rise from the nest of black silk sheets ready to search the best dance floors for a limb-shaking Donna Summer and Grace Jones groove. She'd float through the gay bars like the Queen of the Dark, scattering air-kisses to the coke-snorting DJ's with golden tans. She would leave them and come back to his side, her nose red, her mouth parted in a half smile.

He often felt conflicted, out of his element, but followed her anyway into every strobe and bass throb, unsure of whether his position was her boyfriend or the man who held her coat while he endured the ever-frequent clumsy come-ons smiling boys paid him. In thrall of her repeated lipstick stained bon-mots, he'd pay for another round from his thinning wallet. Trying to keep up, he still found himself taking an inordinate pleasure in watching the beautiful heads turn as she straddled the pulsating floor, repudiating each leering glance to finally take his arm when it was time to leave.

She liked her kicks short and sharp. Liked the fever and the damage done. Liked the reckless sex, binge drinking, and cocaine from white envelopes consumed one jagged line at a time. Liked the sudden shouts of I hate you, the slaps without prompting, the slamming door before the tearful reconciliation. He was hardly pure, either. He realized he was playing with matches just to hear the sound of the sulfur flirting with the spark. He tested; being rougher than he was, telling her she was nothing but a NYC whore, threatening to stop bankrolling the treats she begged for.

As many times as he threatened, whatever indulgence she offered him, he'd accept as enough to seal their bond, if not their fate. He'd return from the work-a-day world to find her with legs spread, fingers idly caressing her constant private pleasure. Sometimes, intoxicated by the mix of perfume and menstrual blood that filled the dark, he'd even indulge in the fantasy that she loved him. It was everything he hoped for. Hard with desire, he'd slip out of his shoes and slip into the unmade bed, to map the small terrain of her back with kisses in search of softness.

"Bring my horse," she'd say, "bring me my pretty pony. Tie him up. Come on, baby, let me mount." It was all gibberish to him, this voice of panic and need, "Oh, the spurs jingle, jangle, jingle – I want to be riding, baby, I'm so happy when I ride." Out would come the foil, the room all in a hush. Out would come the needle, the spoon, the silken tie. One promise of *this is the last time* after another. She'd leave the bed long enough to stick Sinatra or mid-period Miles Davis or Nina Simone on the stereo.

That was their ritual – he'd do her first and sometimes take a taste for himself. He was not proud that he rode that horse... but wasn't it true – what was good for the goose was good for the...? He knew where she'd been – which was a lie. He was always careful, and she was – what? Clean? He made an excuse every time he looked at the hollow tip of panic as if wishing were enough. He'd wrap her tenderly in his arms, jazz filling lingering hours, and they each drifted through their very separate Heavens or Hells.

He never promised to be faithful. Neither had she. Never promised, never asked for anything more than she would turn to him in her need. Even so, he never expected to stray in Detroit. Three Chekov sisters named after the three Virtues met and wooed this unsuspecting man of ambition with a very dry martini. Three witches they were, sans fire burn and cauldron bubble. By light of a televangelist call for contributions and repentance, the welcoming sister who was not Faith or Hope, took him to her bower with a promise that she would open his surprisingly scarred heart.

Took off his shirt, loosened his belt, let his pants slide away into the accepting silence of one who knows when nothing should be said. How he came to Charity did not matter, except in her thrice-charmed bed his nerves sang happiness like no drug he ever tasted, his body returning to elemental warmth again. Light the cleansing sage. Pour forth the healing oils. Yes, he said and yes again, she held him until they were spent. He told himself that in baptism there was neither guilt nor shame, but he still burned with a guilt he could never confess.

He returned intent on being done with needful want, but when he saw her on her knees, puking and shaking, his resolve faltered. She called it disaster, asking some vengeful god's forgiveness. He would never speak of Motor City. In the shambles of an apartment, their feckless desire entwined with the secrets they held and had given birth to some dammed Bukowski poem. More a detached observer than a devoted servant, he heard her beg him to ease her pain. Yet this pain was not needle borne. Time collapsed like an imploding dwarf star, crushing everything in its gravitational pull.

Each vomiting morning moved them closer to the swelling belly. Knocked up. He was going to be a father to spite himself. What kind of man he could be was a cross cut roar of sharpened thoughts as to how unready he was for progeny. And yet if that was the path before them, he would take it. Not a chance, she proclaimed. Even in her worst nods she used protection. But wishes are not facts. A hole in the dam and the mighty swim upstream, unfettered, triumphant. As any casual examination of the diaphragm revealed, her protection had failed.

She declared that there was only one option. He was not asked for an opinion.

Drive, she said. Drive, he did. Changes were now required. Ending one condition precipitated the ending of another. Her distant father was reluctantly brought into the picture. He immediately took charge and paid for her treatment. It would be a few months, but the answering machine picked up his careful reminders that he cared or wanted to see her. He'd come by the recovery center and she'd be in group, or private counseling. These were considered positive signs. An improvement over weeks the phone was off the hook. Weeks she wouldn't leave the depression bed. He still paid her bills.

One unusually warm Tuesday in January he opened the door to find bare walls and empty floor. All hope stolen in the turn of a key. So finally gone, even his clothes had departed. Pulled out without warning or good-bye. In the contemplation of straight whiskey, he realized that was not quite fact. Prophecy has its place. She'd given him a watch for Christmas. A Boy Scout watch with an official Scout insignia stamped on the red plastic box; inside a fire engine red face with white numbers. Inscribed in chrome on the back housing, the Boy Scout motto: "Be Prepared."

He could not remember who first used the word vampire. It almost made sense. Not in the "cast no image in the mirror" trope of old black and white movies, but in a "once heard, true enough" way. An elegant stranger arrives from a foreign land, lavishing attention on the chosen victim who in turn is mesmerized. A vampire must be invited in. He had certainly done that. Invited her in, accepted her beguiling logic. When she recoiled from a silver cross on a chain he tried to give her, he exchanged it for a cameo of a wolf's head.

She hadn't sucked blood, preferring instead to drain his vitality, hollow his will, and deplete his finances to augment hers. Yes, there were times she had bitten him. Broke the skin; licked the red trickle coursing from his hand or chest. Whispering as she did that he tasted like he needed more iron. He laughed it off as he staunched the flow. If only he had used a stake through the heart to mark the death of love.

It might have satisfied his hate, but it was his heart that bore the unquenchable wound when she flew into the night.

The thought he had done everything for her was an iceberg on a brooding sea. He felt defeated, picked at the festering scab of her abandonment. How could he not see she was draining him of everything that had made him? Why had he stayed all those months? Detroit should have been the exit sign. Spreading photographs on the floor he crawled from one aching memory to another. He pissed away duty, obligations to the job, and friends. He let anger distract him from getting out of the lease on an apartment he was paying for but could not enter.

The infection was larger and deeper than he'd imagined. Memory entered his veins in a hot rush like the shimmer of dark wings beating back God's mercy. He could not remember if he called Charity or if she called him, but one day, the three sisters stood at his door. Come to lift the curse, cast out the demon regret. Sat him in a chair and laid hands on him, while singing dead languages to life on their tongues. Plunged him into a lavender bath, wiped his body with eucalyptus, white cotton, black silk, fed him beeswax honey – and left.

Even this did not work to recover his balance, and he went from bad to worse. If the departed was small and dark, the next was tall and blond. If the last year was shadow, he was sure this future was a bright flame. Never thought himself a moth circling her giddy heat. They met at a street dance, sweat and the rhythm of old school R&B. Got slapped for kissing her at Palmer's, but every woman he had been with did that. Got 86'd, then rolled and tumbled the first, but not the last time, on his office floor.

She left her husband. She told him she would have done that with or without him in the picture. He was a catalyst. He never mentioned the vampire to her. He took Polaroids of her wearing nothing but thigh-high leather boots. It was a different kink. He wrecked the car when she gave him a blowjob like the one in Leonard Cohen's Beautiful Losers. She didn't bite it off. He climaxed when the stop sign smashed the windshield. She moved to Seattle, invited him to come from time to time. What friends he had left suggested therapy and turned away.

He did not think it strange when she asked him to wear her father's motorcycle jacket. He could make room for new fetishes. Seattle was that kind of town. Not one china plate survived one session of lovemaking that began on the kitchen table. Every scream was matched by a thrust and her red nails furrowing his back. When the carving knife appeared, it didn't take a blind mouse to know what came next. Small cuts, three times for binding. It hardly bled, but oh, the thrill of the bright blade and the glint in her too-blue eyes was new.

One afternoon the bathrobe sash was torn away, the silk stocking on the doorknob put to use. She begged to be tied to the bed. She cried tears of joy. He stayed hard. They would work it out, this reckless happiness. She did not think it strange to schedule appointments with the therapist every time she thought they might make love. It was something to talk about. Good advice is often after the fact. Fact is the evidence of circumstance. Every time he thought to leave, she'd ask him to book a later flight, offering passion to force another delay.

He called Charity to share his joy. She told him she had dealt the tarot. The Fool lay across the Magician. The reading was all wands and swords. He was courting a red witch, Charity said; had he learned nothing from their ministrations? He said that was jealousy speaking and he had no time for their witchy ways. He hung up, thought better of it, called her back to apologize. Mercury must be retrograde. Gather some sage and smudge the bed. Find some salt and lay a line at the doorsill. Make a circle of protection and come home tomorrow.

One afternoon she threw his suitcase out the window and told him to follow it. He checked into a hotel and in the time it took to unpack his bag, she'd come knocking at the door to ask him back. He didn't return the key. Their love-making was everything right in the world. Her screams muffled as she bit his hand, his pain swallowed, her joy, this had all happened before and would happen again. The knives again, short and sharp, long and lithe, just what was needed for filleting fish, or cutting a vein. Hers, his, and finally, theirs.

The simple pine box his friends asked for was suitable. A closed casket was called for. There were rumors about whether he deserved it. The Chekov sisters were in somber black. Not many knew details, but the Virtues did. When people spoke, they used words like unfortunate, tragic. Don't count the cuts. There are too many. Count the ones that mattered – neck, lungs, heart, wrist, lungs again, and that other one, the thing reminiscent of *In the Realm of the Senses* or Lorena Bobbitt, depending on your cultural preference. What could he have seen in her? Or she in him?

Nearly a year passed before the Queen of Dark heard the now old news from someone she hadn't seen since leaving the Midwest. Turning her cocktail glass to signal the party was over, she tried to remember why she knew that name. Someone she had dated once, she supposed, some fevered fling she'd long-since flung. No one consequential, or surely she would have heard before this. It might make an amusing footnote in her autobiography. With that thought, she turned from the mutual acquaintance to the young man seeking her favors. She asked him to buy her another bone-dry martini.

An Inquiry into the Life of the Count of St. Germain

I HAVE BEEN CALLED immortal, though that term is a misnomer for I had a beginning as we all do. I was born in a small village, isolated from despoilers and marching armies by a girdle of mountains. My parents were no better or worse prepared for the crying and shitting of an infant than any other human who copulates and suffers the consequence of copulation. Though unlike other whelps littered by her, I did not perish at birth or in the womb, and so my mother forgave the suffering of childbirth to dote upon me as her only son. This was long ago, before the comforts of modern medicine, when to live was a blessing or curse depending on the luck of clan and class, geography and state. My generation and geography were surely mixed.

As my parents were not nobility, the prospects for my life were that of any other child in our village, which is to say:

short and brutish. It made little difference that my father was a priest; he worked the fields of our small village with the other men sun up to sun down. This was in the time of the schism of the Byzantine tradition of Christianity. On each Sabbath, my father offered up the prayers of that faith, sprinkled with superstition and the precepts of the old gods.

I was a son of sturdy stock, wed to land and seasons. I grew as every boy in my village, finding diversion in what few games might be played between gathering eggs, milking the goats, or the seasonal butchering. This work was my father's lot and would be my own when I had grown, an unbroken rhythm. Until one curious day, when my life, or rather, my participation in life as we knew it, changed.

I was playing with other boys in an open field that day. The thaw had come and the smell of the grass rose up after the long winter. The green was thick with energy, so much so, that if you put your ear to the ground you could hear life itself pushing up from below. You could hear the hiss of the snake slither, you could hearken to the bunch and spring of the rabbit.

We boys were chasing a rabbit with sticks. If we caught it, there would be meat on the spit that evening. So engrossed was I with the chase that I did not see the clouds gather or the lightning bolt that struck me – once, twice, then thrice – as if kissed by God's own hand.

The boys I played with fell in that field and I alone stood looking to the Heavens, limbs a-tingle and the world bright with sparks that seemed to shoot from every branch and blade of grass. My mother found me with twilight fast upon us after my companions ran for help. I was still standing as if a statue. They carried me rigid to home where father laid a cross upon my head. Fearing I was possessed by a devil, he first sprinkled me with holy water and then tried to drown me (or the devil that possessed me) in a sop bucket.

It failed when my mother intervened. I was placed on a pallet, where I lay unmoving for nearly a full cycle of the moon. With the arrival of the full moon, I finally sat up and asked for something to eat. Life had returned. Those who believed I was possessed and those who believed I was the recipient of a miracle both put these notions aside, and they fed me and sent me to fetch wood.

I was by common reckoning eight or ten years old at the time. This happened in the year you might number 547 by the Gregorian calendar, during what you would call the Dark Ages, when Rome was but a shadow of its former imperial glory and the Church was ascendant – or at least it claimed to be.

The thought that I could even fix a year is curious, for in those days what passed as an annual calendar was some combination of Julian dates and the feast days of the church. In truth, the notion of passing time was a conceit for those who did not know the seasons. What was time to my village? Sun up and sun down, the cycle of the moon, the round of seasons – planting when the thaw came, tending that which could be tended in the heat of summer, the harvest when each fruit or grain was ready, the cutting of wood for the long, cold nights. And so I came to fix the date in retrospect, some 1000 years later when the Roman Pope declared a unified calendar for time liturgical and historical.

That I was touched by the fire of heaven was never in dispute. It was the true beginning of my changed, but not charmed, living. Struck by blue lightning and frozen in time I seemed. All about me; mother, father, playmates, grew wrinkled and frail, either withered with age or struck down by plagues which seemed to arrive as frequently as the dark of the moon, all while I retained my rosy-cheeked bloom.

It was not that I stopped aging. In the fourteen hundred-plus transits of our Earth 'round that blessed star which shines without judgement upon all, my appearance has changed so very slowly. What appears upon my face to you as a mere weeks' worth of wrinkle or line, is actually the result of decades of time passed on my part. I might have lost count of my years, were it not for the grief I have suffered, witnessing the losses extracted by History's cruel whims upon the average man or woman. The world's rise and fall wrote itself over and over again, and my imperceptible growth to manhood condemned me to hide repeatedly in new lands. Always the stranger arriving without paternity, I would be forced to leave before the question of why I did not age as others would be put to me. The rule of thumb – I could spend ten years in one place, twenty at most, before the suspicion of witchcraft and possession would arise.

I will tell you this, after the Enlightenment and the great revolutions of the 18th century, the questions of the spiritual flaws that were considered witchcraft and possession were finally put aside, at least in most countries. However, the questions of scientific causes that might replace them would be as vexing for me if they were asked.

My father observed that I grew not and wished to protect me from rumors of possession and witchcraft which could infect the village gossips. He ordered me to leave for my own safety. He sent me to live with a cousin where I might serve as a stable hand. After the death of that cousin, from there I was packed off to a different relation on the other side of the mountain, one for whom I aged enough in chronological years to be his father or grandfather, even though I still looked as a foundling child not yet in puberty.

This is how the first hundred years passed with my barely aging five years in appearance.

I was, by turns, an orphan, an apprentice, and finally an acolyte, who entered into service at the great monastery of Athos. I learned to read and write Latin and Greek there. In taking the monk's robe with silence as Rule, I could easily spend another hundred years and did. I eventually left Athos rather than be ordained for an eternity as a priest. Once removed from these austerities, the pattern of generations returned. I served as scholar, teacher, and traveling surgeon, or, rather, what passed for doctoring in the years of the first and second Crusades. I learned to arrive by stealth in whatever country I was in, and through observation I would find work that did not require explanation of my past. In each place, a new round of learning was required of me; to learn the language, to learn the customs, and to learn how to remain unobserved and unquestioned as much as possible. I heard more than anyone might imagine and spoke only as much as was needed. In my journeying with Marco Polo, and again in the court of Louis XII, these talents of keen observance and rectitude made me invaluable as a courier, spy or diplomat, as the circumstance and service I was in dictated. My objective was always to keep my head – both figuratively and literally.

What matter that my riches might have come by dint of stealth and diplomacy? From the first to the last, in the service of this monarch or that, such employment conferred a title and paid well, but more importantly, it provided refuge that excused my foreign ways. As often as I was asked how I came to know so many languages and customs, my answer was a deflection to luck or education, depending on the education and status of the one who inquired. The coin I paid to obtain my skills was minted from secrecy demanded by my birth and roots and forged in the necessary veiling of my comings and goings in any given society. The crowns I bowed to in any given land or era were interchangeable in my eyes, for one court's manners and gossip were like another, except for the particular hunger for power that marked the ever-present intrigues that I disdained.

I came to my senses after the wars of religion, when Catholic and Protestant took tooth and claw to killing in the name of Jesus. There was still the French Revolution and the great world wars ahead. Unimaginable in my childhood were means of killing that improved Death's reach with every campaign. But even so, the breadth of bodies planted in a field for the sake of this kingdom or that power has always been the mark of humanity and the source of its shame.

I have seen so much of the pestilence that is the mark of human violence. Before the first machine gun raked no man's land, I was already deaf in one ear and blind in one eye from the blood of wars. I swore it was better to return to the land and seasons, away from the cries of the innocents. Having seen the future and having known the past, I rejected spycraft and diplomacy, whose sole purpose is to fill the pause between conflicts. I rejected the riches and prestige of court life and became what I am today, a gardener. I till the fecund soil, bringing bright blossoms forth and sweet fruits from seed to table.

I am content to be as an oak, rooted and welcoming of those who would seek comfort in my shade. Indeed, I might be the only man alive who has planted an oak and lived long enough to harvest the lumber of the tree. Would that I could plant on oak or olive tree for every death I have witnessed, I would reforest the whole of Europe.

At this rate I will have witnessed two thousand or more years of killing before I finally appear ready for the grave by your measure. Let me assure you, there have been many times I have thought to hasten my demise, if it were not for my curiosity as to what would come next. Next? To remain curious I would have to deny so much of what I knew, but still the desire to find out if there were ever an end to human folly has served me well.

Yes, curiosity looms large even for one who has lived through Enlightenment and revolution. I have seen the rise and fall of monarchies and despots with such regularity that I swear I can smell the turning of history's pages while walking the street, as sure as the scent of bread baking or the aroma of coffee brewing; which was, in fact, how I made my second, or perhaps it was my third, fortune.

Ahh, coffee. It has been my true companion from the moment it found its way to Europe in 1660 until this very day. It was coffee that took me first to its source and back again, to the clamoring shops where silken and brocaded dandies eagerly waited for the well-made cup. As often as ships would sail and with each ocean crossing, my love for that particular intoxication of the senses grew, as did my purse. Real coffee sharpens the senses, and I know well the value of remaining alert.

———————

What might we say about Isabel, the Count St. Germain's wife?

Beauty is far too small a word to hold her symmetry and grace. When she enters a room, it is like a wave rolling upon the river bank; the waters of that space are stirred, and rise in the swell of her movement, the surface embracing green reeds shakes them, moves them, then leaves each glistening with remembrance of the passing. Heads turn, conversation stops.

All these things happen when she is present and yet, if you were to describe her, you would say that she was not plain, but neither was she unconventional in her charms. Her beauty is in the eye of the beholder, a chimera, and while not the kind of woman that photographers would seek for magazine covers, she is the kind of woman that makes the heart swell and the font of desire to flow in her presence, merely to receive her smile.

Her hair is of intermediate length, the dark tresses falling to the midpoint of a long neck in haphazard curls. Her lips thin, the nose thin as well, set like an exclamation point between her eyes as green as November grasses, perhaps shading towards gray, her cheeks smooth. Her body slender, with lean muscle in her limbs – a confirmation of that strength was in her stride and gestures. I will tell you that when she speaks it is the lark announcing dawn. Her voice is the whisper of pines on a summer night. To hear it is to hear those river reeds sigh in the water's embrace.

Do you see a contradiction here? How should I explain the effect of her in motion, of the great power she possesses, which she would say arises from a love for this Count so intense that it projects a beauty beyond the physical? Or would you ask how a woman who can turn heads, one who sparks envy in women and desire in men such as to make them weep at the thought of her embrace, could be married to a man who himself seems at every turn to want to be invisible?

There are those who might think, *What ever could she see in him?* He, of the broken body, with only one good eye and one good ear? A gardener by his own confession – of medium height, physically muscled, as those are who work with the soil. Rough hands and leathered skin from exposure to the wind and sun. He looks to be in his forties, and he walks like a man with the weight of the world on his back. He is like his beloved Isabel in that he both is, and is not, handsome. If you were to study him, you would find a charm that is grounded in knowing, and that he possesses a dignity and calm that disarms.

In speech he is as measured as she is garrulous. He is soft spoken but direct, as if he had abandoned the need of adverbs and adjectives long before and ceded the brunt of conversation to the woman he is clearly infatuated with. They are well paired in that neither seeks the attention of celebrity, yet neither would they deny their capacity for it in an observer's second glance. They invite you to stand close, and they create an offering of intimacy and charm in even the simplest of pleasantries. Their eyes are for each other, and in that you wonder what holds them to their devotion.

If you were to ask her, she would say their bond is the marriage of grief. And after your disbelief, if you pressed her for the meaning of such a statement, she would immediately assess whether you will accept the truth she is about to reveal or whether you will repudiate her account, and turn the inquiry to a corpse. Often enough, she answers that the Count had lost love many times before he found hers.

In the love of two who know the truth about each other and have not turned away, there is no other choice but to obey love's power and love's command. By her reckoning, Isabel is the Count's seventh wife. Unlucky number seven, she might say. Unlucky enough to love an immortal and to marry him, knowing full well she will enter the grave and return to dust, in the very truest sense of that phrase, long centuries before he will cease to be.

She regretted she was not his first love. That honor fell 900 years ago to Beatrix, in the country of some mad king, the name of whom the Count does not remember and which Isabel cares not to know. It was from this union with his first wife that his grief was born; stillborn, she thought. This grief doubled through two sorrows. The first, that he would father no child by his own issue; and the second, that any woman he loved could die from any one of a thousand maladies or injuries before he would age a single gray hair. He mourned Beatrix a hundred years before he could even think to take another bride. The second wife, Fatima, was taken from him with such dispatch that she never had to look at his youth with steadily clouding eyes. After her death, he thought it better to vow celibacy.

Time makes a mockery of human plans. More so the vows of those who live centuries, and even the most hardened heart will succumb to that ripened pomegranate of a girl or this handsome boy who does not realize his own value. And so, it was his luck and blessing that a twice-blessed woman of wit and endurance set her sights upon him and betrayed all sensibility to make him hers. That was Isabel's tale – that the moment she saw him she knew she would not be satisfied until he presented her with the first fruits of the garden of earthly delights. And though he was long-practiced at patience, she was practiced as well and matched her persistence with a formidable and beguiling charm.

Their courtship was measured out at ten years. First the one, and then the other, confessed they could not bear the thought of separation, while the other maintained a careful distance testing the lover's resolve. Eventually, they claimed their promise of one and only, each unto each. By the time they married, she was willing to accept any truth he offered, and he found such joy in her company he could not imagine leaving it.

On their wedding night – and yes, those years that led to it is another story for another time – on their wedding night, knowing who he was, Isabel asked him two questions and told him that he only need answer one.

Who am I to you, my dearest shadow? she asked, and *What are the names of those who have been to the bridal chamber before me, that I might know with whom I share your beating heart?*

And he did answer both questions, and he did share with her such detail that they wept the night to dawn. When the naming was done, she knew the price of the great clouded jewel that was his love and the strength of his faithfulness.

———————

Ahhh, my Isabel, what you ask may bring you no joy, but you deserve to know how you came to be my last love.

Do not jest husband, for you will live centuries while I shall perish like the roses trestled outside this window.

It no jest but instead the summation of these many centuries of searching for that love which would consume my soul. I often thought my Beatrix was that one, for all those who followed seemed to pale beside my love of her. Now I know my first love was truly but a prelude to the desire I have for you, Isabel. You have stolen my heart and replaced it with your own. Give me a kiss for strength, and I will name all that prepared me for your gift, but I will ask you not to judge, nor to question, but to bear silent witness of our vows as I make this account.

Kiss him she did. A long, soft kiss that barely brushed his lips, but imparted her breath into his mouth as if it might quicken his tongue. He lay back on the bed and closed his eyes as if to fall asleep, though it was not sleep so much as some sort of trance in which he propelled himself back through the whole of his life to arrive and be named for what it was.

Beatrix. She was the first, the raven-haired daughter of a builder of churches, halls, and the occasional castle. Master Tiberon, more to the point, was the re-builder of castles after they were burned or sacked, and in that vocation, there was much work to be had. As much an architect as a craftsman, her father was gifted in the art of placing stone one upon another into great arching vaults, and he worked with as many as ten apprentices learning his art at a time. I was in my second month of service to Master Tiberon when she first saw me. In appearance I was maybe 17 or 18 years and well-muscled. I was handsome at that age, or at least handsome in Beatrix's eyes.

Though I had lived nearly 500 years, I was still a virgin, as least in appearance. Not that I didn't know or hadn't seen every way in which a man and a woman, or a man and a man for that matter, might celebrate the flesh. In the brutish custom of the times, I had been physically taken to satisfy need or lust or fear by both men and women, but I had yet to give myself over to the singular passion that we called love. In that, I was a blossom still green on the vine.

I felt my heart stretch and expand under her touch. She wooed me as only a girl ripe for love could, and I her, with all the innocence of a man who hungered for and yet had not yet tasted that first fruit of true love. Our courtship was brief both for her sake and my own. Unlike the usual custom, at 16 she was a virgin true and would remain so until marriage if her mother and the always present nurse had anything to say about it. In fact, they had everything to say about it, and Beatrix plead her desire to marry me, first with the nurse, who then plotted strategy to win her mother's approval.

I was not considered a good match in her mother's eyes, for I had neither land nor dowry to offer. Marrying me would mean that I would inherit not only the daughter but the family's treasure as well since they had no sons, but Master Tiberon liked me and blessed his daughter's union with me. I was so smitten that I neglected to tell her my secret before the wedding, and even afterward, until it could not be kept any longer.

And how did that happen? Isabel asked.

He opened his eyes and put his finger to his lips. Isabel blushed and put her own finger to her lips, then settled back on the bed, her shoulder and hip lightly touching his.

In that time, I thought that I might yet be able to father offspring, and though we tried with all the quickness of rabbits in spring, she never bore a child. It was a grief for her and for myself, as I suspected the very force which gave me immortality had robbed me of progeny. Then one day, not more than can be counted on the fingers of two hands, her father was killed when rains washed out the soil beneath a church wall and it collapsed on him. After that, by rights and custom, the work and the family fell to me.

It was as crushing a blow to my spirit as that wall had been to Tiberon's body. I was not equipped to be the Master, for I had neither the knowledge nor the skill. Moreover, I appeared too young to be respected by those who a moment earlier has been my equals. I could withhold the truth from Beatrix no longer and that evening I confessed everything to her, thinking that the shock of her father's death might temper her shock at knowing my state.

I could not have been more mistaken. My truth-telling actually amplified her tears as she looked at me and saw, for the first time, not a youth near in appearance to her own years, but the unbearable weight of 500 years of survival. There was a look of such remorse and contempt in her visage that I turned away. I regret leaving that room to this very day.

You know the scene in Hamlet when Ophelia slips the mortal coil? Perhaps the Bard got it from me. It's all right – you can laugh, Isabel. I have to. In the space of three days, my life and love were completely stripped away – the father was killed, my beloved entered the cold water from which there is no returning, and I turned to do what I have done so many times before and would do again. I left under cover of dark. In the morning I took passage on the first ship leaving the harbor.

Standing on the deck I thought I would throw myself into the sea but wasn't sure I would die if I did unless I was swallowed by a leviathan. My tears were enough to raise the sea itself as I thought about the loss of my Beatrix.

Isabel reached over to take his hand and placed it on her cheek so he could feel her own tears. The Count took a deep breath and continued.

That ship took me east to Constantinople, and for one hundred years I continued to travel; to the land we now call Lebanon, then by sea again to Egypt, and then west to Morocco. All the while I mourned. Often, I came to the gates of this city or that place of worship just before or very soon after the armies of God would appear. Whether in the name of Jesus or Allah, their arrival meant that inevitably blood would flow.

In 1190 the third Crusade was underway, and my grief ebbed like the tide. Fatima, a beauty who was as much my guide as my companion, buying and selling in the souk. She proposed that I should marry her then, as much for my own protection as for hers. I resolved to tell her my secret right away and I did. She accepted it as the blessing of a merciful God, though I could find no grace in it. Fatima was more a pragmatist than I, for she did not expect to be long lived. As I did not know how long I would live or if I even could die, I bowed to her wisdom and we entered into the joys of the day.

She was right in her expectation. We had been together for only a single year when on a voyage from Tangiers to Cyprus, she was swept overboard in a raging storm and disappeared. I came to view both love and life itself as a curse that I must endure – for I did not have the courage to test the proposition of whether I could die. I traveled then to the furthest regions north as a seaman to tempt that so-called merciful God, which she had believed in and which I had forsaken, into casting me into the watery depths. As it was, I lived on.

In 1343, I took Christina as my third wife. Though I had resolved to tell her before we married, I was called away on some fruitless bit of business and arrived back in Lyon the night before our nuptials. We were married without my having spoken my secret. For the sake of her happiness I bit my tongue and prayed, in my fashion, for the best.

She was the kind of jolly red-haired girl that Botticelli would happily paint in another thirty years. If only she had had another thirty years. I took her for a wife not out of love but for safety. Even after three hundred years, I was haunted by Beatrix's spirit. Still, I had again come to the place where it was more prudent to be wed than not.

We were married four, maybe five years before the great plagues ravaged Europe. Death was all around us, and the rotted corpses caused even those who would call this "The End of the World" to question God's judgment. I too suffered the malady, and yet I did not die – though the pain was terrible. Christina did succumb, and mercifully the end was quick. I carried her body with its swollen limbs and glazed eyes to the already heaping cart of remains and putting my shoulder to the wheel, I rolled it from there to the fire. Once at the cart, there was nothing for me but to continue to carry the dead to ashes. If I could not die, I resolved at least to be of some use to those who did.

So many died in the space of seven years that afterward I could travel anywhere and be accepted as a marvel to have lived at all.

By 1510 I was in the employ of Louis XII as a diplomatic courier, and perhaps if I am truthful, often enough as a spy in the courts of the Bavarian and Hapsburg interests. Agnes was a tall thin courtesan who sought to better leverage her position by taking my hand. This was as much a marriage of convenience for the both of us as not, and one in which I came and went from France to Italy for a period of a half-dozen years.

Again, I had wrestled with the question of when to tell her and what to tell her. My silence had cost me two wives, though the plague was not a result of my silence so much as the abetting of it.

Once again, circumstance demanded that I confess my truth or leave. The Protestant Reformation arrived before I had the chance to reveal my truth to Agnes. By that time I had seen enough of the bloody Crusades, the Inquisition in Spain, and the panic of the plague years to know that the impending wars of religion would be terrible. I would not say that Agnes had gotten religion, but the dour countenance of Luther and the Papish reactions to him were a far greater threat to her than my suggestion that I was nearly a century old.

She thought I was joking or that I was mad. She could appreciate the likelihood of the truth of the first, though she thought it a bad joke. She considered that she might tolerate the second option of madness, as long as I could continue to afford her the trappings of court. That it was some kind of a trick to avoid remaining at her side was a thought she did not want to consider.

Then one morning she looked in the glass and realized that while she was aging, I had not changed a whit from the day that we met. She began by throwing a goblet at me and proceeded to plates and finally came after me with the carving knife, all the while screaming that I was the Devil and I should return to Hell. The fact was that I would not age had become indisputable for her. Her fading beauty now muted whatever advantage she had sought in marrying. No amount of money or clothes, jewels or silk shoes that I might offer would remove the condemnation of age. Seeing neither opportunity nor necessity for reconciliation, I left her.

Then came Julian. He was a surprise, for though I had many companions in those many years, his was the first affection that stirred my heart more deeply than my loins. I tell you Isabel, he was as beautiful as any angel, with bright green eyes, a gaze like a cat's, and a smile to go with it. His hair a halo of ringlets and his hands, oh, his hands were made to play the harpsichord. Such a beautiful soul in the lean frame of a youth who knows he is wanted. Innocent is too good a word, for in truth he knew his inclinations and mine better than I did. Where I was tentative, he was reassuring. Where I discovered my own last dregs of shame, he would have none of it. It was, as he said, Versailles.

Ours was a marriage of the spirit wrapped in the carnal pleasures of the body. In appearance I was not yet 40 and had store enough of the world's goods to look better than I was. I did not ask if he was faithful and I did not expect it. He was too much of this world to resist the temptations of the flesh. I, who was too much of the history of the world, repeated with Julian the kind of life I had shared with Agnes. I came and went, often for long periods. When I arrived, he was there waiting, delighted to take me in his arms and minister to my every need. I would return, looking the same, but he never noticed or perhaps he pretended not to. When I was gone, I was a celibate as I had been those centuries before in Athos. The fleeting pleasures of the body had lost their charm and even the corrupt pleasures were only as good as the singular passion that I shared with him.

She turned on her side and draped her arm across his chest, moved her hand to the base of his penis as if to stroke it, then thought better and brought it back to the space just above his heart. She looked at him but said nothing. He saw the look as both understanding and forgiveness, though the latter was unnecessary. In fact it was not forgiveness, for she knew as he did that it is not the gender of the lovers that requires forgiveness, but rather the ways in which we fail to express love.

I was in the Swedish Court when the news of the French Revolution came. There was both excitement and foreboding – the fear that some new contagion might find its way north. Others congratulated themselves for being nobility in a tolerant northern country, and pointedly told me they were glad to rise above France with its libertine inequity. I said nothing and even as I hurried to leave. I knew there was no point in returning to Julian. As the revolution spiraled from the first sudden blush of *liberté* and fraternity, to a bloody struggle for the power to send one's former companions and now one's enemies to the blade, my return would only endanger us both. At that moment in France, I would be seen as the infection that must be excised from the body politic. And if Julian were not alive, there was no point in returning.

That is how I came to America for the first time and saw it after its own revolution. New Orleans culture felt familiar, and its location was a suitable home base for repeated trips north on the mutable Mississippi river to the thin wild spaces between the march of the Europeans and the complex cultures of native nations, which that very expansion of settlers ignored, betrayed and replaced. With the coming of the war of the states which was hardly civil, I returned to Europe, only to find yet another war, the Franco-Prussian campaigns.

My dear Isabel, this recounting wearies me. Not that you don't deserve your question answered. Even this brief telling brings forth that which I would deny, that the constant of my immortality has been the dance of Death harvesting those we love and those we hate and those we do not even know in ever greater numbers.

He turned his head away. Whether he was simply pausing or silently weeping she could not tell. Then he began again, in a voice barely more than a whisper.

Had I passed as a natural man when struck by that bolt, my brief life would have been seen as a gift to my parents and the way of life flows. Having lived as I have been fated, I now see the way of the world is only war and pestilence, with the gifts of love so few and fleeting as to be lost or forgotten in that carnage.

She tenderly stroked his cheek.

Dear husband, please – you do not have to continue. I have heard enough.

He took her hand off his cheek and kissed the palm.

I promised an accounting and so I shall continue, for while the deaths will go on without pause, even to the turning of the last century's page, there is but one more wife, one last love to name before your own gracious self. Mirabelle was her name.

I met her when she fled from the bloody suppression of the Paris Commune in May of 1871. Wounded, she fell into my arms and I carried her away from the fighting to my garret in the crowded quarters of the old city. I tended her wounds and kept her hidden while the national army massacred thousands of men, women and even children for participating in the socialist dream. We had no recourse to a priest; to any who asked, I claimed her as my wife, who was suffering from a form of consumption that required her to remain bed ridden. It was a poor story, but it sufficed for the year it took before it was safe enough for us to leave France.

In the unfolding of our lives, this lie actually became true, for in that year Mirabelle did fall ill. At the time, it was deemed to have been the result of infection from her wounds. Now, if it had been diagnosed in these times, her disease would be recognized as cancer. Our move to Spain gave no improvement, and she died in the summer of 1873. It was there that I planted an olive tree over her grave, the first of the hundreds I have planted since.

After Mirabelle there has been no one until you, my Isabel. These are the ones I mourn to this day, the ones who will share our bed. I wish I could forsake their memories for you, as I have the hundreds of people who I have known and who have died since my childhood. For so many, their living and dying was little more to me than a day with sun and clouds. It is those few who took my heart, and in the taking, hollowed out life itself for me until I was no better than a walking ghost among ghosts, not dead and yet not living.

When I read books where immortality reigns, they do not come close to knowing the terrible weight of watching all that you love die century after century. Yet I remain, and all that is history passes compounding my solitude.

She took his face in her hands.

My beloved, you must have a tremendous heart for having seen what you have seen and heard the cries of innocents lost to those who would love them. I shall live until I die, and until then it will be my joy to provide for you in every instance, holding that great heart as my own and your grief as mine.

With that, she kissed him tenderly and they turned to embrace each other.

Before dawn entered the chamber, she rose from the marriage bed and went to the kitchen. She took rough milled flour, yeast, and salt, and set to making bread. Rise it did but not for long before she beat it down, shaped it and took it to waiting oven. While it baked, she ground the dark roast coffee beans, brewed a pot, then took out the lavender honey and sweet cream butter. Out of the fire came the bread and placing all on a tray, Isabel returned to her beloved.

Eat, husband, for this is our union. This broken bread, a marriage of salt and flour and life itself, is us. This honey collected from bright blossoms is our love. The coffee's dry berries ground and steeped – our grief. Taste these and know how good we are for each other.

It was enough for the Count to be in the garden and she to be true to her word, to do everything to make this day an invitation to his happiness. From that moment on, though they were wedded in grief, they lived as if every moment of joy, each meal, each embrace, each day would be entirely theirs, both their first and their last.

One day Isabel came to the Count and said to him:

You might be 1400 years old, my dearest man, and know all the truth which history does not put in books, as well as the cycles of seasons and the promise of the soil. You still know nothing of the truth that lives in the hearts of women.

What matter is that to you, madam? You are the only woman whose heart I desire to know.

I am graced by that intent, but dear husband, for all our years, you still do not truly know my heart. Sit here with me and I will tell you a secret. One which is a dark rose, with petals as purple as a plum and edged with a red as bright as my own blood. Sit and hear how I planted and tended this secret. At this moment, when it is now ready to bloom with fragrance so heavy... it will drive me mad if I do not share it with you.

You have my attention, the Count said, settling into a straight-backed chair.

No, not that one, she said. You will weary of sitting long before I finish. Come here to the bed and I will wrap my arms about you and whisper my secret as gentle as the dragonfly caressing the pond lily.

With that, he rose and settled again. True to her word, she laid her head on his chest, stroked his ruddy cheek, and began:

I have long considered the problem of our marriage. No, husband, do not speak for as I sat silent on our wedding night it is not your place to object to the thought that there is a problem within our bond. Simply listen to me for now. We both know that one of us shall live and the other die. You have been through this fact six times already and each time the grief of loss has driven you to madness, solitude and a sorrow that would consume the world were it given a form. You confessed this to me on our marriage night as you told me of those who proceeded me in this marriage bed. My heart broke for you with that telling.

For a year now, I have thought to spare you that grief again and have come to the conclusion that I should find my successor, and thereby assure your happiness before I die.

That is impossible, he said, for you cannot be replaced. I will not allow it.

She shifted her weight, curving to bring her flanks in line with his, spooning him and with one hand gently pulling his buttocks against her hips as if she were going to grind her sex against him.

On the contrary my dearest, it is not replacement but rather continuation that I am seeking. I propose to find for you a woman like myself, my twin as it were, or one as close enough in looks and temperament, in speech and manner, in touch and compassion that you would think I have come to live another 50 years, In this way, I hope to postpone that which drives you mad in favor of that which is the madness of our love.

He tried to roll away to look at her, but she tightened her grip and leaned so close it seemed her breath entered his ear and left his nostrils.

I do not believe there can be such a woman.

You are mistaken. I have already met her though you have not. Just as you might graft a rose, I will graft her unto myself until we are of one mind and one purpose.

Does she know? Has she consented to this intrigue?

She does not know you except by reputation and by having seen you in the gardens. She has no knowledge of your antiquity but she knows me, or at least thinks she does. At present, we relate to each other in sisterly fashion, but I believe she can feel the stirring of a deeper bond.

Soon I will take her as a lover might, by degrees to the recesses of my heart that I might begin her instruction. If I am right, by the time I bring you to the bed, she will be ready for every secret to be plumbed. She will open herself to you for my sake even as I am opening myself to her for yours.

Can I not dissuade you from this course?

You cannot. Trust me my dearest one, that if this is to fail, it is not because you stand in opposition to me but that my love for you is so consuming that I will undermine my own intent.

One morning Isabel woke from a curious dream so perplexing that she immediately dressed and went in search of the Count. She caught up with him at the gate as he was leaving to plant olive trees on a hillside above the town. Catching his arm, she gestured for him to sit. Once they were settled, she recounted the night's gift:

I dreamt that we were giving a party. Perhaps it was a wedding reception? In some ways, the gathering seemed to be our own, but this one was held in the village great hall — or maybe it was the church? The space had the shape of the church, except there was a short-walled pool where the baptismal font normally stands. I'll come back to that in a moment, but I must tell you that this party was held in the evening and many of our absent friends were there, as well as townspeople and people who I did not personally know, but that you did. These seemed to be friends from the past — courtiers and ladies in waiting, monks, academics. And once I glanced at you and you were looking at a woman. She could only have been Beatrix. I also saw you another time gazing at a handsome youth, who I took to be Julian. For each, you held such a look of love and longing on your countenance that, though I have never seen an image of either lover, I was sure they were in attendance.

The hall was decorated in a curious way. The length of the hall was hung with columns of differently colored silks – black at the entrance door, then purple, then a blue the color of the night sea, then a blue like the sky at harvest, then a dark green that shimmered with a lighter green interwoven, giving a feeling as if spring were giving way to summer. Then an orange, followed by a sunflower yellow, almost gold in look, then a white silk, and finally, at the far end, a red silk curtain which obstructed the view of the choir loft where an orchestra played music. Set between the columns were rich tables laden with food – bread, meats, bowls of fruit, cakes with marzipan frosting or spun sugar roses, and vintage wines. Bordeaux, pinot gris and pinot noir, cabernet, oh, and even a golden mead that was so fragrant you could smell the meadow as you held the glass! There was no table to sit at or chairs, so the people mingled freely from one table to another and couples danced in the open spaces.

The pool was elevated with a tile enclosure that went from light to dark and back again, seemingly without beginning or end. In the pool, water and a mix of lily pads and lotus blossoms floating on the water, all illuminated from beneath the surface. Above the pool, there was a giant trout suspended without a visible means of support. It was as if the trout had leapt from the pond and remained frozen in midair, its spine arched in an upward curve, mouth open as if to swallow a fly. I could not tell if it was fiberglass, or carved wood, though its detail was such as to suggest an actual trout, twenty-some feet long and floating in air.

You and I were walking from one end to the other, and we would stop to chat with the guests and pour or sip a glass of wine. Along the way as we met or passed various women, I kept asking you, do you like this one? You said, not now. You turned to me and said quite directly, as you do in waking life, will I not give up this foolishness of finding you another? But in the dream, it felt quite urgent that we agree on who would be your consort. Then I looked around for Janine but I did not see her.

Janine? So that is the name of the one you would have me take...

Maybe it is. What does it matter? It was the name of a woman I wanted you to meet in the dream. It was at this point that the most interesting part happened. I really wished I knew what it stood for, but I don't have a clue, so I'll simply describe it. You can tell me what it means.

As we were near the end of the stroll, you walked over to the pool and touched the flank of the fish. It bowed. That's the only way I can describe it, the head came down and the tail rose up, and from its mouth came a shower of sparks cascading to the floor like it was vomiting some great firework. Sparks cascading all around our feet, but we were not harmed, there was no heat, nothing burned. You reached out a second time and touched the head of the fish and the shower of sparks stopped and a trickle of red liquid began to pour of out of the fish's mouth into the pool. There was a glass in your hand, and you filled it from the stream and then raised it up in a toast to the guests, to the orchestra, and to me, then drank it. You offered the glass to me and when I put it to my lips I tasted the most wonderful wine.

What was surprising to me was not the miracle of wine pouring out of the fish's mouth, but rather that as it poured into the pool it seemed to have no effect. The pool did not discolor or rise. The wine did not cease even after you invited the guests to partake of what you called the blood of Heaven.

I don't know how long it took as the guests began filling their cups, but it seemed that we were speaking with someone when the music stopped. Three great horn blasts sounded, and a drum roll began. You turned and held up your hand and called out, "the trout" and then as the drums beat faster, the guests took up the call – "the trout," "the trout," "the trout" – until you touched the great fish a third time and it dove into the pool. I could not believe anything so large could enter anything so small and yet the twenty-foot fish went into the water, disappearing entirely. The pool did not overflow with the displacement such a massive body would command, but seemed to absorb it entirely, leaving only a ripple where it entered the water, which gently lifted the lily pads and laid them back to rest again.

What could it mean, dear husband?

In the old stories, Isabel, a fish – often a salmon, some-times a flounder, but a trout would do – was the source of wisdom. It could foretell the future and bestow wishes. What would you wish for my Isabel?

That you and I could be alone in our bed.

He picked up an olive seedling and looked at the green branch that would someday bear fruit and replied to her. Really? Only that?

I have tried, but I am a selfish woman. For these many years I have shared the bed with you and with six others as well. They may not be between the sheets in body, but they occupy the chambers of your heart and in your grief, you keep them alive. No, not even that. They do not live, they are ghosts that cannot leave. For your sake, I cannot cast them out. As much as I wish an end to your sorrow, I want to have this too-short time with you for myself alone. I foolishly think I might extend our love by finding another who I might mold in my own image and likeness to be with you when I am gone.

The Count had heard this kind of complaint before. Not from Isabel, but from Mirabelle, just before she departed Paris for Spain. She had not put it as Isabel had, for she had never known how many lovers he had embraced before her. Mirabelle told him that she felt he still shared his marital bed with whoever had come before, sometimes even saying that they shared their bed with Death. In this she was right; Death was a constant, silent companion, and had walked with the Count for more centuries than she might imagine. And for her sake, he determined that he would banish Death, both from their bed and from their household.

It was good for a year until her body turned upon itself. In her pain, she refused to eat or drink until Death entered the moonlit room to embrace her. Afterwards, the Count stood on the balcony of the room, holding Mirabelle's still-warm flesh, now stilled as he called out to the night, "You are back again, dammed pestilence. You are not even worthy of being called a whore, so easy and cheap your satisfaction. Religion, politics, greed, honor; you come in the name of any cause and every flag, and tonight you come to steal that which I would never give up. Though I would gladly relinquish all my days to bring her back, you, craven Death, would refuse to accept my offer."

It seemed to him that even as he left one landscape after another, one profession, one disguise, one lie for each and every generation, Death had journeyed with him. He might pack and flee under the cover of night, but Death was there to greet him. It made no difference if Death rode behind a cavalry sword or musket, on the back of a tank or machine gun, it was never enough. Even the ovens and mushroom cloud were not enough. Death was always wanting more.

The Count put down his shovel and looked at Isabel. He thought he should say something more and yet the fact was she knew him as well as any mortal ever had. She could read his every thought in the way he sat or stood. It seemed to him that the grace of sun and sweat, the sound of the shovel making space for life, and the wind stirring the grass – all these humble powers would give him time enough to consider if anything more could be said.

I am going now to put these trees to root and while I am there, I will think on your wish. When I return, I will tell you what I have decided.

With that he kissed her on the cheek and turned to the path. She stopped him before he could take a step and turned him around to face her once more.

I will have you hear me, dear Count. Know that I will bear any pain for the sake of our happiness. If what I propose can add one day to that delight, it is worth doing. Even as you plant trees as a gift to the future, I am planting this thought with you for ours.

———————

The Count returned as the sun dipped and caressed the western horizon. Stripping off his shirt, he went to the basin Isabel had left on the small table beside the door. He poured some water and washed his hands, slowly, examining the scars that had accumulated over the centuries. He wet a cloth and washed his arms and chest. As he reached for the back of his neck, Isabel came behind him and took the cloth out of his hands. She washed his neck, shoulders, and back, interspersing the slow strokes of the washrag with small quick kisses before handing him the clean shirt hanging next to the door.

Husband, will you sit with me?

He settled into a chair and cleared his throat.

Isabel, I have considered both of your propositions, and would offer a counter to each.

What might that be?

She asked as she poured him a cup of coffee leaving room for the warmed milk and sugar that would follow.

I am thinking that I should go before you.

Go before me? Husband, can you die?

That is an unanswered question. I have been shot and stabbed, drowned or close to it, but always came back. Broken bones and disease have touched me many times, even the Black Plague refused me, while it took Christina. We both were laid low in the grip of the pox, but while she went to the charnel house, I pulled the very cart that held her stilled lips.

The notion that the curtain should fall came again to me while planting trees. I have considered my own demise before, though I always resisted acting on it. However, while I considered your scheme to cheat my grief upon your inevitable leaving of me, this time I thought why bother? Truly I have lived long enough. Even curiosity thins, and this jury-rigged frame that is civilization shows through. Are there any surprises left?

He laughed, then continued. As in those movies about "immortals" we watched with such disdain, I suspect that were I to lose my head, I would not recover.

She smiled at the thought and replied to him. I will not take your head. Besides, I seriously doubt that there would be flashes of power or that the gift of deathlessness would flow to me. I wouldn't want it.

You might for my sake. Take my head. On the other hand, the end finally came to that reputedly immortal Scottish prick, the Bad Lord Soulis, when he was wrapped in chains and boiled in lead. Would you rather take that approach?

She took him in her arms.

But if we were to do this, to end your grief by ending your life, it would be the start of my own sorrow, a sadness I could not bear.

What I would propose is that we would snuff out the candle which is mine first and then if you were brave enough, you could take away your own bright light that we might be consigned to the fire together. As the priests used to say, Ashes to ashes, dust to dust. Then into the darkness or the light of next.

To be with you, I would. But how, husband, might this be accomplished?

Poison?

Surely you joke. It might be a path for me, but poison will leave your head in place and your disposition in as foul a mood as I might imagine.

You could smother me with a pillow.

And how long would I have to hold the pillow to your face? An hour? A day? Until the limbs stop twitching or the flesh falls from the bone? And who will hold the pillow to my face?

Isabel put her cup down and stirred the coffee with her little finger.

What way might assure that we will both go into the hereafter, together? If you want me to agree to this end, it must be, in a word, foolproof.

I will conceive of a means that will be by my own hand, Isabel, and once accomplished, you may do as you wish. Or if you are so resolved to be my wife in death as in life, a means must be found that will take the two of us hand in hand.

And now dear husband, it is my turn to ponder whether to accept your proposal or go forth with my own.

He stood at the table and mimicking her, stirred his coffee with his little finger.

To each of our plans and our considerations. We shall circle around the cup of intention to see whose will is stronger.

In unison they exclaimed –

Why yours, of course!

———————

Each went about their living as if nothing had changed. The Count rose from their shared bed in the morning and worked the day. The grapes on the vine embraced the sun, the olives darkened in the heat. At some point of every day he would look at the fecund earth, forgetting his age and his grief, focusing only on the moment before him. The thought of ending anything seemed absurd. Once spoken, however, the competing thoughts gathered strength from the denial. Life could not go forward unaltered.

Some days, Isabel went into the village to find Janine. Not every day, though, for she wanted to have their time be anticipated and appreciated. They talked, they laughed, they shared secrets. They did what women everywhere must do. The small, dark haired girl shared her longings and fears, and Isabel offered a ready ear and encouragement, making her younger companion blush at the thought that she had Isabel's confidence.

They were together so often that soon enough, the village gossips were jealous and shocked by turns. No one would say anything to them directly, but as the two women strolled the market arm in arm or leaned over an espresso at the cafe, heads turned and their happiness was noted.

One afternoon Isabel stood behind a wooden straight-backed chair in Janine's tiny apartment massaging the young woman's shoulders. On the table before them were two glasses with the last of the bottle of wine. Isabel leaned in, her loose ringlets brushing the back of Janine's neck.

Have I told you that I love you?

There was a moment of silence. Isabel's hand stroked the bare shoulder and trailed up Janine's neck to lightly pinch her ear lobe. Janine turned and kissed her.

Not directly, but I have suspected it for weeks now. Say it again.

She took Isabel's hand and brought it to her waist as she stood and turned to embrace her.

You know how these things go, or if you don't, you should. One blush leads to another, one kiss to another, and then one hand begins to remove that which separates us from our desire. It makes little difference who is first, for the bed welcomes both. Day turns the clockface to the wall. There is then only the tangle of legs, only the slipping of hands and tongues into Now, and afterward, the moment when the truth would out if only the right question were asked – along with an equal prayer that the question would remain unspoken.

On that afternoon Isabel wondered if there could be life without the Count. As soon as she thought it, she was ashamed. He would never leave her. She would have to leave him or accept his proposal that he die before her if she was to be only and truly with Janine.

She turned to look at Janine and saw herself as she was before she met the Count. Again, she was ashamed as soon as she entertained the thought, for she knew that when she had first seen him, she had wanted him. It did not matter his situation – married, single, gay – she could only think of how his kisses might taste and the feel of his arms holding her as she shuddered her climax. Now she wanted that same feeling of another's kisses and another's welcoming arms, with that same determination not to be denied.

Sensing her thoughts, Janine lifted her head from Isabel's shoulder.

Is something wrong my love? You shuddered.

It is nothing...

To be true to love, one must speak what one fears might end the promise of happiness. She then thought to herself that she understood now in a way she had glossed over before, how the Count could be caught between wanting to share his secret and not wanting to break the spell of two alone together, here in this blessed Now.

He had told her his secret the same night that she had asked him if he wanted to marry. He had kissed her with such sweetness that even now, years later, her lips trembled at the memory. He had said to her, what price would you pay for happiness? Any price, had been her reply. Would you be willing to die for it? Yes, she had said, wouldn't you? And his reply was, I cannot die for happiness for I have lived 1400 years without death and without the joy so many arrive at, without realizing what a treasure it is. She did not think it a joke but a terrible tragedy that in all that time he had not known happiness, and said if I can give you that which you long for, I would die that you might have it – even if it be only a single year of the joy I find with you.

This thought brought a tear to Isabel's eye and Janine seeing it, asked, what do you desire above all else?

Above all else, oh Janine, that desire would be to share my bed with the both of you without anger or jealousy. She began to laugh. The kitchen is another matter...

The Count? You and I, and your husband? *Ménage à trois*?

No, not in the sense of the three of us in a sex act, or not only in every kind of sex act three can conceive of, but as a holy trinity, the Font of Love. I am selfish enough to not want to be denied you, but I cannot be denied him. What I desire above all else, is that we would be together as the blessing of all that is good for as long as I may live.

Though Janine said that it was a very sweet thought, and though she kissed Isabel first on the forehead, then on the lips, and then on each of her nipples, on her belly and on her sex, she did not know the meaning of that desire. How could she? Isabel herself did not know the import of those words, for she could not see that Death had entered the room and was welcomed once again.

———————

Janine is going to come to the house tomorrow. That's what Isabel intended to say to the Count as she made her way back towards the house through the old town's dusty streets. She was happy at the thought. Before they would ever come to embrace his proposal of finality, they would test hers of continuity. She was sure that once Janine was with them, the Count would see all the ways she could extend his happiness.

Just as she was crossing the bridge, a black Mercedes rounded the corner and skidded on the narrow span. The right front fender caught Isabel's shoulder bag with the meats and cheeses she had gotten at the market and spun her into the side of the car just behind the front door, knocking her back against and over the rail into the river far below. The hams flew one direction, the cheeses another, Isabel a third.

There was a splash but she did not hear it. She did not feel the pain of broken bones or water entering her lungs. What she saw was an enormous fish swimming towards her. She thought she had seen it before – or perhaps not. It was large but not as large as the image in her head, but there was no time to sort out what fish was which. The fish circled under her and rose so that she felt its moving form against her breast. Instinctively she brought her arm around the fish, clutching it closer.

The great fish heaved and took a course towards the surface, carrying her with it. Isabel was astonished at the speed of the ascent towards the light and struggled to hold on. As the trout hit the surface it seemed to float upward, slowing down and coming to a stop, suspended in the air with Isabel still clinging to it. It was timeless and still. She felt at peace, unconcerned that this was either a violation of every law of physics or some kind of dream.

Gravity took hold and the fish fell back into the river. With the splash, Isabel released her grip and floated just below the surface.

The chief of police delivered the news. He found the Count in the half-lit tool shed sharpening a scythe. He cleared his throat and said simply, your wife has died. It was an unfortunate accident.

He expected to hear something, a cry perhaps or at least a question about how and when. There were neither. The Count simply looked up and then sat on an overturned box and put his head in his hands. The Chief could not tell if he was crying, though his shoulders shook. He inquired if there was anything the Count needed, anything he could offer him in this time of loss. The Count said nothing, but waved him away with one hand as he rubbed his forehead with the other. The chief thought it best to give him his privacy and left.

Two days later he came back to see how the Count was faring. The door to the house was open. Inside, everything was as it should be. The furniture was in its place and books were on the shelf. The dishes in the cupboard, food in the refrigerator, even the bed made. Clothes were hanging in the closet and neatly arranged in the dresser drawers.

But the Count was not at home. The Chief believed that he would be back soon. He had to return, for Isabel's body was ready to be claimed. Surely he would want to bury her. But he did not return, and a day or two later a woman named Janine who was reputed to be Isabel's lover came to make arrangements for a cremation.

It seemed as if the Count had disappeared entirely. The Chief's efforts to locate him or even to find some evidence of how he might be contacted – an address, a phone number, an e-mail address – proved fruitless. When he made further inquiries, he was unable to find any record of a passport and the national identification card on file appeared to be a forgery. There was no birth certificate.

It was as if the Count St. Germain were a fiction. He was, the Chief concluded, a man who did not want to be found or did not have a past.

Story Notes

Fishhook

George, Henry & Marguerite

Memorial Day

These three stories are based on oral histories that I collected in 1981 while I was the Humanities Scholar for northern Minnesota.

Radio Daze

I first developed this story for the Minnesota Fringe Festival performance of 1967. It was based on my stint as a morning radio DJ while I was in college.

Remodeling the Kitchen

My nephew Jason Oftel told me a version of this story while he was showing me his newly remodeled kitchen.

Eve to my Adam

This story is a fictionalized account of an experience a friend had in graduate school.

Barbeque Bus

I first created this story for a 1988 Halloween show by Bad Jazz, a performance art trio with Michael Sommers and Kevin Kling, at the Walker Art Center in Minneapolis.

Wooing Constance

John Zeller told me a version of this story on the way to a friend's wedding.

Then

This narrative is a combination of two improvised stories. I performed "B-O-B" for the ghost story concert at the 2000 Illinois Storytelling Festival, and "The Devil in Tennessee" for a 2001 performance at the Uncommon Grounds coffeehouse in Chicago.

Tongue of Angels

A New York Times article on the burning of library books during the 1992-1996 siege of Sarajevo was the inspiration for this tale.

Gas Stop

I began creating this story while listening to the Eagles' "Hotel California." It is a nod to the Chinese, Japanese, and South-east Asian tradition of telling stories involving sex between humans and ghosts.

Meeting Myself

I was re-reading Ray Bradbury's "The Sound of Thunder" when I came up with the idea for this story. In hearkens back to the traditional time travel stories of twentieth-century science fiction.

The Ghost in the Machine

The works of Wittgenstein and modern neurological research on language and cognition inspired this offhanded tale.

Dating the Vampire

This story is a fictionalized account of two bad relationships I had in the 1970's. A variation on the "vampire" half appeared as part of my Fringe Festival performances of "Moby Dick Tonight!"

An Inquiry into the Life of the Count St. Germain

I found a note in my journal about a New York Times article that I read sometime in the 1980's. According to the article, the allegedly immortal Count Saint Germain had been seen in Berlin. The question I asked myself was "What would immortality actually be?"

About Loren Niemi

Loren Niemi told his first formal story when he was in First Grade to the disapproval of Sister Mary Margaret and has been at it more or less nonstop since then.

For the last 40 years he has been an innovative professional storyteller performing, directing, collecting, coaching, and teaching stories – traditional and personal, funny, scary, erotic or poetic – to audiences of all ages in urban and rural settings.

He tells the life he lives frequently, artfully, and truthfully.

He is the author of the award winning "The New Book of Plots" on the use of narratives in oral and written forms and the co-author with Elizabeth Ellis of the critically acclaimed "Inviting the Wolf In: Thinking About Difficult Stories" on the value and necessity of stories that are hard to hear and harder to tell.

What Haunts Us is his first published story collection.

He was a 1998 Bush Foundation Leadership Fellow and the recipient of a 2016 National Storytelling Network's Lifetime Achievement Award.

His website is at **www.lorenniemistories.com**.

Also From Moonfire Publishing

<u>Written in Blood</u> by Sheila Marshall and Scott Stenwick. David Killian is an ancient vampire with the power to write the fate of the Northland in his own blood. When he writes the ideal lover and companion into life, he summons artist Kristie Slay from Chicago to Castle Danger on the North Shore of Lake Superior. Kristie is drawn by the town's mystery and the surprise of a new love springing from her past. But she carries with her a hidden secret that may lead to both their undoing.

<u>Ipswich</u> by Scott Michael Stenwick. This sequel to Scott Stenwick's 2009 debut urban fantasy novel **_Arcana_** tells the story of Sara Winchester, a young heiress and newly-empowered magician. With the help of the centuries-old order of magicians known as the Guild, she explores the mystery of her mother's untimely death. On her travels she must face a killer who can control the spirits of the dead, and the remnants of an order of dark magicians who seek the Guild's destruction.

<u>Go Fork, Ye Crooked Spoon, and Let Me Live My Knife!</u> by Sheila Marshall. This whimsical guide to cooking and carving meats is both educational and entertaining. The book is written in Shakespearean language and includes amusing quotations (and almost-quotations) from the Bard. It is filled with striking illustrations by Sarah Marie Wash that complement the instructive and sometimes irreverent text. This book is a must for every kitchen that holds William Shakespeare and his works in high esteem. Learn to cook and carve, with hearty laughs all the while.

The Zombies' Guide to Dining by Moonfire. Let's face it – you can't just eat all brains, all the time. There comes a point where you need some variety in your diet. In this amusing follow-up to The Vampires' Guide to Dining, author Moonfire moves on from vampires to the world of zombies, outlining their personality types and suggesting recipes for their unique anatomies. Like the previous volume, the book is filled with humorous illustrations and plenty of new ideas for navigating the world of the undead.

The Vampires' Guide to Dining by Moonfire. Everybody knows that vampires don't drink wine. But what do they eat? In this humorous cookbook and compatibility guide, author Moonfire explores the world of dating and hosting the various personality types that make up the vast legions of the undead. The book is filled with funny and imaginative illustrations, and is a perfect handbook for undead-themed party planning.

Keep In Touch

"...and this is the domain of the strange, the Marvelous, and the fantastic... Here is the freed image, dazzling and beautiful, with a beauty that could not be more unexpected and overwhelming."

Moonfire Publishing seeks out the strange, the unusual, the macabre, and the unconventional, and our titles reflect that vision. Check out our website and join our mailing list.

www.moonfire-publishing.com

We are always on the lookout for new manuscripts that take a fresh approach to magical realism, fantasy, science fiction, horror, the paranormal, and related themes, including humorous treatments of these genres. If you are interested in submitting a manuscript for consideration, please see the website for the submission guidelines.